Determinants of Credit Spreads

Corporate Finance and Governance
Herausgegeben von Dirk Schiereck

Band 6

PETER LANG
Frankfurt am Main · Berlin · Bern · Bruxelles · New York · Oxford · Wien

Arne Wilkes

Determinants of Credit Spreads

An Empirical Analysis for the European
Corporate Bond Market

PETER LANG
Internationaler Verlag der Wissenschaften

Bibliographic Information published by the Deutsche Nationalbibliothek
The Deutsche Nationalbibliothek lists this publication in the Deutsche Nationalbibliografie; detailed bibliographic data is available in the internet at http://dnb.d-nb.de.

Zugl.: European Business School, Diss., 2010

Cover Design:
Olaf Glöckler, Atelier Platen, Friedberg

D 1540
ISSN 1869-537X
ISBN 978-3-631-60604-9
© Peter Lang GmbH
Internationaler Verlag der Wissenschaften
Frankfurt am Main 2011
All rights reserved.

All parts of this publication are protected by copyright. Any utilisation outside the strict limits of the copyright law, without the permission of the publisher, is forbidden and liable to prosecution. This applies in particular to reproductions, translations, microfilming, and storage and processing in electronic retrieval systems.

www.peterlang.de

Foreword

While the question of what it costs a company to raise debt capital in the form of bonds on the capital market has occupied the minds of financial researchers for decades, conclusive answers have yet to be found in many areas. This is accompanied by the fact that the highly significant global financial crisis has sustainably relativized the expertise gained in the past. This observation also particularly applies to the issuing of corporate bonds in Europe where the market has not yet achieved the maturity of the US market and continues to be influenced by national aspects. Corresponding to the market maturity of the US bond market the geographical research focus has been on the US. The currently available doctoral thesis of Mr. Wilkes, who sets out to empirically research European corporate bonds analogue to the findings for the US bond market and in the process presents a whole series of innovative analyses which meet the highest international standards, is in itself remarkable. He finds himself in a strongly competitive, mainly US American environment.

This study approaches the above-mentioned research gap with meticulous attention to detail and utmost care. Its primary objective was to determine the yield spreads (credit spreads) between the risk-free interest rate and corporate bonds of varying creditworthiness of European issuers, using capital market data and information relating to the overall macroeconomic situation and also to define the level of integration already attained by the European market for corporate bonds. This indicates the attainment of an objective state of knowledge providing the basis for the derivation of profound recommendations for action in financing practice.

In his thesis Mr. Wilkes optimally fulfils his self-imposed objectives. The study contains numerous exciting findings and has been written in a way that readers will thoroughly enjoy reading on till the end. I wish this work the broad readership it deserves.

Professor Dr. Dirk Schiereck

Preface

I would like to express my sincere gratitude to my doctoral supervisor, Prof. Dr. Dirk Schiereck. His academic guidance and encouragements throughout the process of selecting the topic and writing the thesis were invaluable for me. Besides providing very helpful advice and instant feedback, he always encouraged me to focus on the economical and practical implications of the rather theoretical topic of this thesis, which contributed to its success.

In addition, I would like to thank Prof. Dr. Roland Füss for assuming the role of secondary advisor to my dissertation. He provided highly valuable input, especially regarding methodical topics of my thesis.

Furthermore, I would like to take the opportunity to thank my friends and colleagues from the Munich Office. My discussions with them and our joint times in the office were extremely enriching and their encouragements were a great motivation to me. Moreover, I am thankful for the support of all my friends in Germany and abroad. On this note, I want to express my gratitude to Tom Gales, who thoroughly proofread my manuscript.

Last, but definitively not least, my deep gratitude goes to my family, my father Alexander Wilkes, and my sister Henrike Kolks, whose moral support during the course of writing my thesis were a great encouragement for me. Finally, I am especially grateful to my beloved wife Anne. Her support, her patience, and her love were invaluable sources of inspiration for me to finish my dissertation. I dedicate this book to her.

Arne Wilkes

Content Overview

List of Figures 13

List of Tables 15

List of Abbreviations 17

1 Introduction 19

2 Study 1: Are European Corporate Bond Markets Integrated? A Macro-Finance Term Structure Model Approach 27

3 Study 2: Has Liquidity Risk for Bonds Increased During the Financial Crisis? A Study for the European Corporate Bond Market 67

4 Study 3: The Short and Long-Term Determinants of Credit Spreads – An Analysis for the European Corporate Bond Market 99

5 Conclusion 127

References 131

Table of Contents

List of Figures 13

List of Tables 15

List of Abbreviations 17

1 Introduction 19
  1.1 Motivation and Objectives 19
  1.2 Definition and Scope 22
  1.3 Course of Analysis 24

2 Study 1: Are European Corporate Bond Markets Integrated? A Macro-Finance Term Structure Model Approach 27
  2.1 Introduction 27
  2.2 An Affine Term Structure Model 29
      2.2.1 Short Rate Dynamics 30
      2.2.2 Diffusions of State Variables 31
      2.2.3 Bond Pricing 32
      2.2.4 State-Space System 35
  2.3 Data 37
      2.3.1 Risk-free Yields 37
      2.3.2 Credit Spreads 39
      2.3.3 Macroeconomic Variables 43
  2.4 Research Strategy and Estimation Results 45
      2.4.1 Interpretation of Latent Factors 51
      2.4.2 Impulse Responses from Shocks to State Factors 52
      2.4.3 Variance Decompositions 61
  2.5 Conclusion 65

3 Study 2: Has Liquidity Risk for Bonds Increased During the Financial Crisis? A Study for the European Corporate Bond Market 67
  3.1 Introduction 67
  3.2 Theoretical Background and Related Literature 68

3.2.1	Pricing of Defaultable Bonds	68
3.2.2	Liquidity as Driver for Bond Prices and Credit Spreads	70
3.3 Data		73
3.3.1	Corporate Bond Sample	73
3.3.2	Credit Spreads	75
3.3.3	Liqidity Measures	76
3.3.4	Additional Control Variables	78
3.4 Empirical Specification and Estimation Results		80
3.4.1	Basis Regression and Overall Impact of Liquidity	80
3.4.2	Structural Break Analysis	84
3.4.3	Sector- and Rating-Specific Results	91
3.4.4	Summary of Empirical Analyses	97
3.5 Conclusion		97

4 Study 3: The Short and Long-Term Determinants of Credit Spreads – An Analysis for the European Corporate Bond Market 99
   4.1 Introduction 99
   4.2 Theoretical Background and Related Literature 101
      4.2.1 Determinants of Credit Spreads 101
      4.2.2 Cointegration Analyses of Credit Spreads 102
   4.3 Cointegration Tests 103
   4.4 Data 107
   4.5 Empirical Results of Credit Spread Dynamics 110
      4.5.1 Results of Johansen Cointegration Test 114
      4.5.2 Results of ARDL Cointegration Test 118
      4.5.3 Deviations of Credit Spreads from Equilibrium 123
   4.6 Conclusion 124

5 Conclusion 127

References 131

List of Figures

Figure 1-1:	Credit spreads on European corporate bonds	19
Figure 1-2:	Development of the European corporate bond market	21
Figure 2-1:	Risk-free zero coupon yields	39
Figure 2-2:	Mean credit spread curves	41
Figure 2-3:	Credit spreads of corporate bonds	42
Figure 2-4:	Macroeconomic factors	44
Figure 2-5:	Factor loadings on yields and credit spreads	54
Figure 2-6:	Impulse responses to the financial factor	56
Figure 2-7:	Impulse responses to the real activity factor	57
Figure 2-8:	Impulse responses to the inflation factor	58
Figure 2-9:	Impulse responses to the first latent factor	59
Figure 2-10:	Impulse responses to the second latent factor	60
Figure 2-11:	Impulse responses to the third latent factor	61
Figure 3-1:	Time series of credit spreads for different rating categories	85
Figure 3-2:	Changes of average credit spreads and average relative bid-ask spreads	88
Figure 3-3:	Changes of average credit spreads and average swap spreads	89
Figure 4-1:	Time series of variables	109
Figure 4-2:	Actual and fitted credit spreads	122
Figure 4-3:	Deviations of actual credit spreads from long-term equilibrium	123

List of Tables

Table 2-1:	Summary statistics of risk-free yields	38
Table 2-2:	Summary statistics of corporate credit spreads	40
Table 2-3:	Parameter estimates of the term structure model	47
Table 2-4:	Regression of latent factors on dynamics of yield and spread curves	52
Table 2-5:	Variance decompositions of yields and spreads	62
Table 3-1:	Summary statistics of corporate bond samples	74
Table 3-2:	Panel unit root tests of credit spreads	75
Table 3-3:	Basis panel regressions	82
Table 3-4:	Panel regressions with structural break dummies	87
Table 3-5:	Parsimonious panel regressions with structural break dummies	90
Table 3-6:	Summary statistics of corporate bond subsamples	91
Table 3-7:	Liquidity effect on credit spread changes for different credit quality and different sectors	93
Table 3-8:	Rating and sector perspective on the liquidity effect on credit spreads	95
Table 4-1:	Summary statistics of variables	108
Table 4-2:	Expected long-term effects of determining variables on credit spreads	111
Table 4-3:	Augmented Dickey-Fuller unit root tests	112
Table 4-4:	Zivot-Andrews unit root tests	113
Table 4-5:	Johansen cointegration test	115
Table 4-6:	Error correction model (Johansen approach)	116
Table 4-7:	Bounds testing approach	119
Table 4-8:	Long-term relationship (ARDL approach)	120
Table 4-9:	Error correction model (ARDL approach)	121

List of Abbreviations

A	rating category A
AA	rating category AA
AAA	rating category AAA
ADF	Augmented Dickey-Fuller
adj.	adjusted
AIC	Akaike information criterion
ARCH	autoregressive conditional heteroscedasticity
ARDL	autoregressive distributed lag
BBB	rating category BBB
BFGS	Broyden, Fletcher, Goldfarb, Shanno
bp	basis points
crit	critical
CS	credit spread
e.g.	for example
ECB	European Central Bank
ECM	error correction model
EGLS	estimated generalized least squares
EMU	European Monetary Union
est.	estimate
et al.	and others
EU	European Union
EUR	euro
GARCH	generalized autoregressive conditional heteroscedasticity
GLS	generalized least squares
I(0)	integrated of order zero
I(1)	integrated of order one
I(2)	integrated of order two
i.e.	that is
IKB	IKB Deutsche Industriebank AG
info.	information
LEH	local expectation hypothesis
LM	Lagrange multiplier
max	maximum
min	minimum

ML	maximum likelihood
mn	million
no.	number
ODE	ordinary differential equation
OLS	ordinary least squares
p.a.	per annum
PCA	principal component analysis
PP	Phillips-Perron
prob	probability
R^2/R-squared	coefficient of determination
RESET	Regression Specification Error Test
SIC	Schwarz information criterion
std. dev.	standard deviation
std. err.	standard error
t-stat	t-statistic
U.S.	United States of America
UECM	unrestricted error correction model
VAR	vector autoregression/vector autoregressive
VECM	vector error correction model
vs.	versus
W-stat	W-statistic
ZA	Zivot and Andrews
Δ	delta/difference

1 Introduction

1.1 Motivation and Objectives

Credit spreads express how markets evaluate the riskiness of a corporate bond compared to a risk-free asset such as a government bond. However, the markets' risk assessment changes over time and thus credit spreads are not constant but vary by time. During the last decade, credit spreads in the European corporate bond market have been highly volatile. As Figure 1-1 depicts, the average spread of AAA-rated corporate bonds has been as low as 17 basis points in March 2002 and as high as 280 basis points in October 2008. BBB spreads even vary in the range of 75 basis points and 618 basis points. Therefore, a detailed study of what drives credit spreads in the European market is relevant and necessary.

Figure 1-1: Credit spreads on European corporate bonds

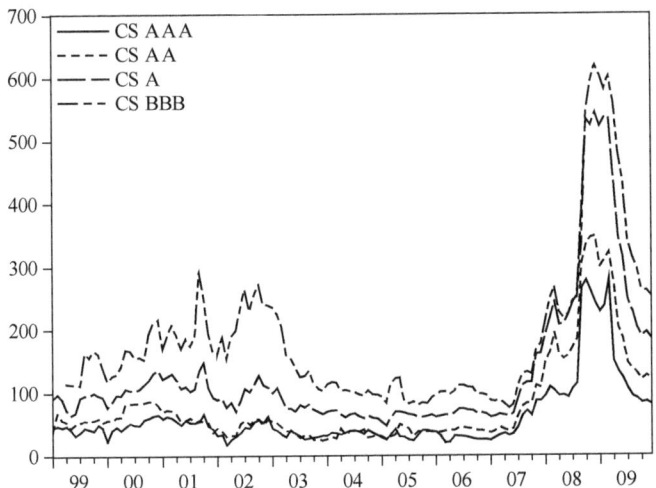

This figure shows the credit spreads in basis points for AAA, AA, A, and BBB corporate bonds of the iBoxx Corporate Index of euro-denominated bonds. Credit spreads are calculated as the difference between yields to maturity of the corporate bonds and risk-free bonds with the corresponding time to maturity.

To know how credit spreads evolve over time and which variables determine their variation is important for practitioners and different stakeholders in the economy. For corporations the credit spread directly determines the cost of debt and therefore the company value, since the capital costs enter as a discount factor in standard valuation models, such as the discounted cash flow method.

Banks generally have a high exposure to the variation in credit spreads, too. On the one hand, banks issue bonds on the capital market to refinance their assets, such as loans or investments. Thus, the credit spreads on their own bonds determine the refinancing costs and the business models of banks. On the other hand, banks hold assets prone to default risk, such as corporate bonds or credit derivatives, in their trading and banking books. In this regard they are exposed to the risk of varying asset prices caused by the changes of credit spreads. The ability to model these credit spread variations is most important for the risk management of banks because the regulatory capital requirements are directly linked to the exposures associated with holding risky assets.

Regulators provide the regulatory framework for financial institutions and set guidelines with regard to capital requirements. Thus, they need a good understanding of the risk faced by financial institutions. In the recent financial crisis, the existing regulatory framework was proven to be insufficient to prevent a considerable number of situations where banks collapsed or had to be saved by governments. Especially the high risk exposure of assets to illiquidity was underestimated and a good understanding of the interdependencies between illiquidity and credit spreads is therefore essential for future adjustments to the regulatory frameworks.

Investors and portfolio managers also have a significant interest in understanding the dynamics of credit spreads because changes in credit spreads lead to variations in asset and portfolio values. Investment strategies are therefore directly linked to the assumptions regarding the expected changes of credit spreads in the future.

Finally, economists and policy makers see credit spreads as an indicator for the economy. Widening spreads reflect an increasing risk aversion towards holding defaultable assets and often indicate an economic downturn. In this regard the relationship between macroeconomic variables and credit spreads give insight into the complex interdependencies between monetary policy, market expectations, and the real economy.

Due to the importance of credit spread dynamics for the financial markets and the real economy, a broad literature covering theoretical and empirical studies on bond pricing and credit spreads has evolved. Many studies have discussed the impact of variables such as the risk-free interest rate, the equity market, or the leverage on corporate credit spreads. However, most of these fail to explain the considerable volatility of credit spreads due to omitted variables or methodologies that are insufficient to account for the observed dynamics. Especially during the recent financial crisis other aspects such as liquidity, the condition of the macroeconomy, or the long-term equilibrium relationship between variables seem to play an important role in determining corporate bond prices and credit spreads.

Furthermore, empirical literature on credit spreads has mostly addressed the U.S. markets mainly because of the depth and the level of integration of the U.S. corporate bond market. Since a common European market has only emerged during the last decade, empirical studies for the European corporate bond market are still rare. However, as Figure 1-2 illustrates, the European market for corporate bonds has grown by over 10% p.a. since 1999. The European corporate bond market, which has almost tripled during the last ten years, has become increasingly important for investors, the private sector, and the public sector alike. Thus, a thorough analysis of the determinants of credit spreads for this market is required.

Figure 1-2: Development of the European corporate bond market

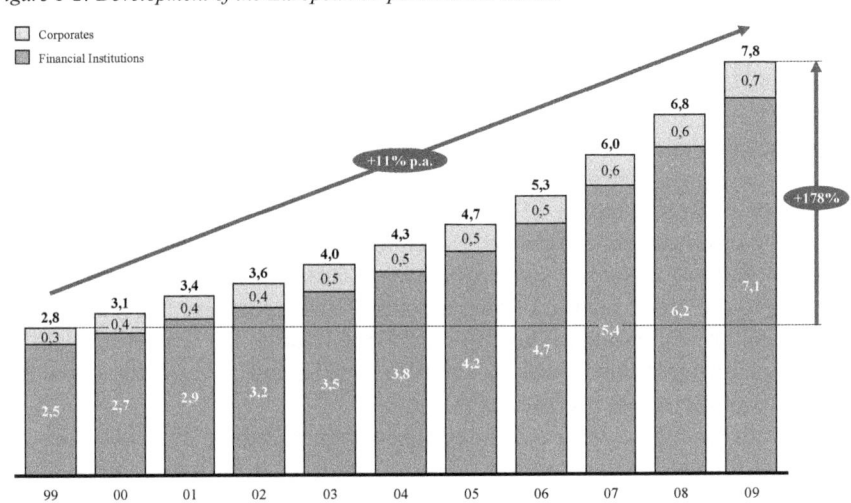

This figure shows the outstanding amounts in trillion euro of fixed income securities excluding derivatives in the euro area as reported by the European Central Bank.

Finally, researchers and practitioners agree that the recent financial crisis has had an immense impact on credit spreads and asset prices, yet existing models failed to predict or even explain the variation in credit spreads after the start of the subprime crisis in 2007.

Overall, this thesis covers many aspects of those unexplored questions relating to credit spreads and the European corporate bond market and analyzes the determinants of credit spreads from different angles and with different methodologies. Specifically, the following research questions are addressed:

1. Is the European corporate bond market integrated, and what are the linkages between macroeconomic factors and the term structure of credit spreads in Europe?
2. What is the impact of liquidity on European corporate credit spreads and how has liquidity risk changed during the financial crisis? Are certain credit qualities and specific sectors more sensitive to illiquidity than others?
3. Does a long-term relationship exist between European corporate credit spreads and their determinants and can short-term deviations from equilibrium be explained by the dynamics of the endogenous variables? How much did credit spreads deviate from equilibrium during the peak of the financial crisis?

1.2 Definition and Scope

Throughout this thesis credit spreads of corporate bonds are subject to different empirical analyses. Thereby the credit spread is defined as the difference between the yield to maturity of a corporate bond and the yield to maturity of a risk-less government bond. In order to reflect the term structure of yields both bonds should have matching times to maturity. Credit spreads are differentiated according to the credit quality of the corporate bond issuer and the credit risk is approximated by the rating of the corporate bond. Due to the limited availability of data on high yield bonds, only investment grade bonds, i.e. bonds with a rating of BBB or better, are regarded in this thesis.

The credit spread, as it is used in the subsequent empirical analyses, does not only reflect the credit risk caused by the probability of default and the likely recovery rate of the issuing company. It also includes any additional premium demanded by investors for other risks, such as illiquidity.

The geographical scope of this thesis is restricted to the European market and more specifically to the euro zone. This implies that the corporate bond samples used for the econometric estimations are adjusted so that only euro-denominated corporate bonds issued by EU companies are included. Macroeconomic variables entering the models also refer to the member countries of the euro area. The geographical scope of the thesis also restricts the time span of the subsequent analyses. The European Monetary Union (EMU) started in January 1999. Pagano and von Thadden (2004) argue that exchange rate risk prevented financial integration prior to the start of the EMU with the result that financial claims were imperfect substitutes. Therefore, this date marks the earliest possible point where a study on the European market as a common market place makes sense.

The choice of the variables that enter the empirical models as determinants of credit spreads is based on a thorough review of the existing literature on bond pricing and credit spreads. Besides standard bond pricing literature on structural models and reduced-form models, more recent approaches to model credit spreads are reviewed. Macro-finance literature, term structure literature, studies on the financial crisis, and cointegration studies, among others, build the background upon which the subsequent analyses are based and from which the theoretical determinants of credit spreads are deducted.

The second and the third empirical study in this thesis specifically address the impact of the financial crisis on the interdependencies between credit spreads and their determinants. Hence, the timeline of the events that led to the global crisis has to be regarded. Brunnermeier (2009) argues that increasing defaults of U.S. subprime mortgages in February 2007 triggered the financial crisis. The effects on the global markets, however, became evident with a delay of several months. The global subprime crisis started with the collapse of two hedge funds of Bear Stearns in June 2007, and the near failing of the German bank IKB in July 2007 initiated the spillover of the subprime crisis to Europe. The results were a dry-up in the market of short-term asset backed securities and a significant widening of (corporate) credit spreads during the second half of 2007, as Figure 1-1 illustrates.

After a short recovery period during the first months of 2008, where credit spreads narrowed again, the collapse of Lehman Brothers in September 2008 triggered the second and more severe phase of the global financial crisis. During the months after that event, credit spreads across all credit qualities increased by 300% to 500% compared to the pre-crisis averages. In contrast to the economic downturn of 2001 and 2002, where foremost credit spreads of low-rated companies widened as a result of increased risk aversion towards default risk, the financial crisis of 2008 and 2009 also hit high-rated companies (see Figure 1-1) and financial institutions.

Towards the end of 2009, credit spreads narrowed again to a level before the Lehman collapse. However, they still remain significantly above their pre-crisis averages indicating that capital markets have still not fully recovered from the global shock of the financial crisis.

1.3 Course of Analysis

Following this introductory chapter, Chapters 2 to 4 comprise self-contained empirical studies and address different research questions.[1] Chapter 5 provides the conclusions of this thesis. The scientific object of credit spreads in the European corporate bond market is the same in all of the three studies. However, the objectives and the methodologies differ, giving this thesis a broad application area and allowing a holistic view of the dynamics of and the interdependencies between credit spreads and their determinants.

The first study aims at answering the question of whether the European bond market is integrated. While the U.S. bond market is widely regarded as highly integrated, the question of the degree of integration has not been fully answered for the European bond market. Several previous studies argue that financial integration in Europe has increased during recent years. However, empirical evidence suggests that some residual segmentation seems to persist.

To approach the question of bond market integration in Europe from a new methodical angle, a term structure model of risk-free yields and corporate credit spreads for the European bond market is estimated. In addition to latent factors, the model includes observable macro factors that are linked to inflation, real activity, and financial activity, thus belonging to the class of macro-finance models. Following the approach of Ang and Piazzesi (2003), the term structures of risk-free yields and credit spreads are simultaneously modeled using yield and macroeconomic data from the euro zone. Comparing the empirical results regarding the market price of risk, impulse response functions, and variance decompositions with a similar U.S. model developed by Amato and Luisi (2006) the study yields that the European bond market is integrated to a significant degree. However, it is concluded that the European bond market has not yet reached the level of the U.S. due to some residual segmentation and market friction.

The second study analyzes the impact of liquidity on corporate credit spreads and compares the liquidity risk before and after the start of the global financial crisis. Liquidity was regarded as major risk factor for asset prices during the recent crisis and the study significantly contributes to revealing how illiquidity has affected corporate bond prices and credit spreads. Thus, implications for banks, portfolio managers, and regulators regarding liquidity as an important source of risk can be derived.

---

1   Adjusted versions of the three studies have been submitted to different academic journals as papers under the co-authorship of Prof. Dr. Roland Füss and Prof. Dr. Dirk Schiereck.

In the empirical analysis of the second study, different panel regressions for a sample of European corporate bonds are estimated. Controlling for a broad set of variables, the study examines the impact of changes in liquidity on credit spread changes. Thereby, both bond-specific and market-wide liquidity are regarded. With a structural break approach the impact of liquidity on corporate credit spreads is then compared between the periods before and after the start of the financial crisis. In addition, the results are differentiated for different credit qualities and sectors. In order to yield robust results the econometric estimations address heteroscedasticity, serial correlation, and fixed effects in the panel of corporate bonds.

The empirical results support the hypothesis that liquidity risk has significantly increased during the course of the financial crisis. The impact of illiquidity on credit spreads during the crisis is especially large for high-rated bonds and bonds issued by financial institutions. Thus, it can be inferred that illiquidity has become an important risk source for asset classes, which prior to the crisis were considered as nearly risk-free in regulatory frameworks and in risk management approaches of banks. To prevent a recurrence of the dramatic impact of the liquidity crises on the banking sector, the study supports the suggestion to revise the regulatory framework by attaching more weight to liquidity risk.

The third study examines the long-term and short-term relationships between credit spreads and a broad set of determining variables for the European corporate bond market. So far, almost all empirical studies of credit spreads only concentrate on the short-term dynamics by regressing credit spreads on different explanatory variables while neglecting possible long-term relationships. Especially during the recent financial crisis those standard regression approaches fail to explain the highly volatile credit spreads and findings indicate that credit spread variations are only partially explained by observable variables. Furthermore, models that omit actually existing long-term relationships between variables yield potentially biased results (Duan and Pliska (2004)).

Different unit root tests show that credit spreads and their determinants are non-stationary during the sample period of January 1999 to December 2009. Therefore, the requirement for a cointegration analysis is provided and the existence of a long-term relationship is tested with a Johansen approach and an autoregressive distributed lag (ARDL) approach. Both cointegration procedures have the advantage of simultaneously estimating the long-term relationship between the endogenous variables and the short-term dynamics of the adjustment process towards the equilibrium relation.

Empirical evidence confirms the existence of a long-term relationship between credit spreads and a set of determining variables. For the first time the few existing U.S. results of cointegration analyses of credit spreads are confirmed for the European bond market. Moreover, the study extends existing cointegration approaches to analyze credit spread dynamics as it examines the simultaneous interactions between a broad set of determinants and credit spreads. In contrast, previous studies mainly analyzed the partial relationships between credit spreads and selected factors, such as the risk-free term structure or variables related to the equity market. In addition, error correction models are able to explain large parts of short-term and long-term credit spread variations and thus provide a significant improvement to existing regression-based approaches.

Furthermore, a comparison of actual credit spreads with equilibrium credit spreads that are deducted from the estimated long-term relationship confirms a significant over-pricing of credit spreads after the collapse of Lehman Brothers in September 2008. A convergence of credit spreads towards equilibrium is only observed towards the end of 2009. Hence, the third study helps to explain the abnormal market reactions during the recent financial crisis.

2 Study 1: Are European Corporate Bond Markets Integrated? A Macro-Finance Term Structure Model Approach

2.1 Introduction

Affine term structure models are based on the assumption that bond prices follow the law of one price, i.e., no arbitrage opportunities exist between bonds with different maturities and otherwise identical risk patterns (Piazzesi (2009)). However, in order for this to hold for a term structure model of credit spreads, the corporate bond market must be integrated.

There is sufficient evidence of an integrated U.S. bond market, but this question has not been fully answered for the European bond market. Prior to 1999, exchange rate risk prevented financial integration, because financial claims were issued in different currencies, traded at different risk-adjusted prices, and were thus imperfect substitutes for each other (Pagano and von Thadden (2004)). Since 1999, however, several studies have examined whether the European bond market is integrated.

Baele *et al.* (2004), for example, conclude that euro area government bond markets are highly but not perfectly integrated due to market liquidity differences. They also found that corporate bonds exhibit a slightly lower degree of integration, despite the fact that the issuing country of a corporate bond has only marginal explanatory power for its credit spread.

Pagano and von Thadden (2004) came to a similar conclusion. They attribute observed yield differences primarily to differences in fundamental risk that still exist among member countries. In addition, they find that a minor part of the observed country spreads is caused by market segmentation due to different trading costs, clearing and settlement fees, or taxes.

Balli (2009) approaches the question of financial integration in the euro zone from two angles. First, his preliminary findings that local risk factors cannot explain observed yield differentials among EMU members indicate full financial integration. Second, however, he uses multivariate GARCH models to show that global risk factors affect government benchmark bond yields differently. He also finds that volatility changes are not homogeneous among EMU members. He thus concludes that euro bond markets are not yet fully integrated.

From these studies, it can be concluded that the European government and corporate bond markets seem to be integrated to a significant degree. Under this assumption, a term structure model of credit spreads is estimated, and the results should be comparable to similar models tested for the U.S. market. However, differences are expected to be found between Europe and the U.S., which can be attributed to residual segmentation in the European bond market.

This study presents an affine term structure model of credit spreads for the European bond market. In their recent work, Taylor and Williams (2009) also confirm empirically that no-arbitrage term structure models can describe term spread variations as a result of shocks to underlying risk factors even during the recent financial crisis. They find empirical evidence that the bond pricing framework of Ang and Piazzesi (2003), which is also used to build the term structure model of this study, describes jumps in interest rate spreads between overnight federal funds and long-term interbank loans during the financial crisis, which began in mid-2007.

This study follows Amato and Luisi's (2006) model setup and definition of variables in order to ensure the results are comparable to theirs for the U.S. market. Thus, the model includes both unobservable state variables as well as observable macro variables as state factors that drive the term structures of yields and credit spreads of defaultable corporate bonds. The structure of the market price of risk linked to the risk factors of the model is analyzed, and impulse responses of shocks to the risk factors and decompositions of the forecast error variances of yields and credit spreads are conducted. Furthermore, this study explores how the latent factors in the model influence the term structure of credit spreads.

This is the first study that empirically tests an affine term structure model of credit spreads with observable macro factors for the European market. The results are compared to a similar model tested with U.S. data to indirectly test the degree of integration of the European bond market. The results indicate that the European bond market is largely integrated. Common risk factors can explain considerable parts of the credit spread variation, even if the results of this study deviate in several aspects from the U.S. results. It can be concluded that, due to residual segmentation and market friction, financial integration in the European bond market has not yet reached U.S. levels.

The remainder of this study is organized as follows: In the next section, the term structure model with the description of the dynamics of the model factors, the required bond pricing formulae that follow a no-arbitrage assumption, and, finally, the state-space representation of the model that allows the estimation of the parameters in a discrete time setting are derived. Section 2.3 describes the data and the methods used to construct the time series for risk-free yields, credit spreads, and the macro factors. Section 2.4 provides an overview of the methods used to estimate the model parameters and discusses the estimation results. In addition to parameter interpretation, impulse responses on yields and credit spreads that result from shocks to the state variables are shown. Decompositions of forecast error variances with regard to the state factors are also presented. Section 2.5 gives the conclusions and discusses ideas for future research.

2.2 An Affine Term Structure Model

Yield curve models have a long history in finance literature. The early contributions of Vasicek (1977) and Cox *et al.* (1985) presented models that used only one latent factor. The literature then evolved to models using more than one latent factor, e.g., Longstaff and Schwartz (1992). Finally, the seminal paper of Duffie and Kan (1996) provided a complete characterization of affine yield models and paved the way for term structure models using several underlying factors.

Until recently, the macro-finance term structure literature primarily covered empirical models of the risk-free yield curve. Several studies have attempted to explain the term structure of U.S. Treasuries based on combinations of macroeconomic variables with affine term structure models that follow the no-arbitrage rule.

For example, Ang and Piazzesi (2003) use two macro factors, real activity and inflation, constructed from various time series. Rudebusch and Wu (2008) present a macro-finance model with a structural macroeconomic specification based on output and inflation, while Dewachter and Lyrio (2006) use output gap, inflation, and the real interest rate as macro variables and incorporate long-run macroeconomic expectations.

Diebold *et al.* (2006) include manufacturing capacity utilization, the federal funds rate, and annual price inflation as observable macro variables. They allow for dynamic interactions between the macroeconomy and the yield curve.

Recently, the literature has expanded to cover default-prone corporate bonds. Several empirical papers aim to describe the term structure of credit spreads of different rating categories for the U.S. market. Amato and Luisi (2006), for example, present an affine term structure model of credit spreads on a sector level, with three latent factors and the observable variables inflation, real activity, and financial activity. Dionne *et al.* (2007) use aggregate consumption and inflation as the macro variables, and apply the Markov switching term structure model of Bansal and Zhou (2002) to defaultable corporate bond yields and credit spreads on a sector level.

Krishnan *et al.* (2007) build a model that explains credit spreads on a firm level using firm-specific risk variables and the macro factors real activity, inflation, stock market returns, and stock market volatility. Wu and Zhang (2005) examine how the observable macro variables inflation, output, and market volatility influence credit spread term structures on a sector level.

For the European market, Hördahl *et al.* (2006) estimate a model for German risk-free interest rates that includes output gap, inflation, and the short-term interest rate as observable macroeconomic factors. Lemke (2008) presents a term structure model of risk-free interest rates for the euro area. His macroeconomic model includes inflation, output growth, and the short-term interest rate as input variables.

Until now, there has been no empirical study that explains the term structure of credit spreads in the euro zone based on a macro-finance setup. Terazzan (2006) estimates a term structure model of investment-grade credit spreads on euro-denominated bonds, but only uses latent factors. A recent study by Rottmann and Seitz (2008) performs a regression analysis on German corporate bonds, and concludes that credit spreads for single firms depend on several micro- and macroeconomic factors. For macro variables, they include the risk-free interest rate and stock market volatility. However, they do not build upon a no-arbitrage framework to explain the term structure of credit spreads; instead, they include time to maturity as an additional independent variable. They find a significantly positive, non-linear relationship between time to maturity and credit spreads, which supports the hypothesis that a term structure model for credit spreads can be empirically estimated for the euro zone.

Finally, Van Landschoot (2004) also analyzes the sensitivity of changes in investment-grade credit spreads to macroeconomic and financial variables for the euro zone. However, she also does not apply a no-arbitrage framework, as done here. She uses regression analysis to estimate the impact of implied stock market volatility, the level and slope of the default-free term structure, and liquidity measured as average bid-ask spread on the term structure of credit spreads, which she estimates using an (extended) Nelson-Siegel approach.

2.2.1 Short Rate Dynamics

This study follows Amato and Luisi's (2006) approach, which is closely related to that of Ang and Piazzesi (2003), in setting up the term structure model. The procedure allows a comparison of the results with those of Amato and Luisi (2006), as well as enabling a link between the differences in the results and the differences between the U.S. and European bond markets. The model belongs within the general class of affine term structure models introduced by Duffie and Kan (1996) and Dai and Singleton (2000). A reduced approach is used to model the macro part, as per Ang and Piazzesi (2003), as the setup does not allow for structural interaction between the term structure and the macro model.

The short rate is modeled as a monetary policy reaction function that follows the policy rule proposed by Taylor (1993). X_t is defined as a column vector, with the first three elements being the unobserved state variables at time t, and the last three elements being the observed macro factors inflation, real activity, and financial activity. Thus, it is assumed that the instantaneous risk-free rate can be expressed as an affine function of X_t:

$$r_t = \delta_0 + \delta_1' X_t \ . \tag{2.1}$$

According to Amato and Luisi (2006), the only differences from a traditional Taylor-type reaction function are the use of composite macro factors and the use of a macro factor reflecting financial activity. Likewise, the instantaneous credit spreads of the different rating classes $J =$ AA, A, BBB are modeled as affine functions of the same latent and observed state variables:

$$s_{J,t}^Q = \gamma_{J,0} + \gamma_{J,1}' X_t \ . \tag{2.2}$$

Note that δ_0 ($\gamma_{J,0}$) and the elements of the column vector δ_1 ($\gamma_{J,1}$) reflect the constant and factor loadings of a linear regression of the instantaneous risk-free rate (instantaneous credit spread) on the state variables.

2.2.2 Diffusions of State Variables

In line with common term structure literature, the state vector X_t, is assumed to follow a Gaussian, mean-reverting diffusion process:

$$dX_t = K(\overline{X} - X_t)dt + \Sigma dW_t \ , \tag{2.3}$$

where W_t is a six-dimensional vector of independent Brownian motions. To ensure the process is Gaussian, the variance matrix Σ is assumed to be constant over time. Furthermore, the elements of Σ are restricted so that the latent factors are orthogonal to the observed macro factors.

K is the mean-reversion matrix of the process governing the speed with which the state variables are pulled back to their long-term means $\overline{x}$. Following Amato and Luisi (2006), K is defined so as to guarantee independence between unobserved and observed state factors. Without loss of generality the long-term means of the state variables are assumed to be zero. Equation (2.3) can thus be rewritten as:

$$dX_t = -KX_t dt + \Sigma dW_t \,, \tag{2.4}$$

which gives the diffusion process for the state variables in continuous time. Note that a discrete version of Equation (2.4) must be used in the state-space system in order to match the model setup with the data set of monthly observations.

2.2.3 Bond Pricing

As Duffie and Kan (1996) show, the price of zero coupon bonds in this class of models takes the form:

$$P_{R,t}(N) = E^Q \left[\exp\left(-\int_t^{t+N} r_u \, du \right) \right] = \exp(A_R(N) + B_R'(N) X_t) \,. \tag{2.5}$$

Thus, the prices of zero coupon bonds are exponential affine functions of the state vector. The first equality in Equation (2.5) establishes the existence (but not necessarily the uniqueness) of a risk-neutral pricing measure. The second equality reflects the concept that bond prices of all maturities can be derived from the state variables X_t. The deterministic functions A and B impose the cross-equation restriction between bond prices of different maturities and ensure the arbitrage-free nature of all bonds.[2]

A similar logic applies to defaultable bonds, where the appropriate discount rate of a bond of rating class J at time t under the risk-neutral probability measure Q is equal to the sum of the instantaneous risk-free rate r_t and the instantaneous credit spread $s_{J,t}^Q$. Hence, the price of a defaultable zero coupon bond at time t, with a credit rating J and a remaining time to maturity N, is:

$$\begin{aligned} P_{J,t}(N) &= E^Q \left[\exp\left(-\int_t^{t+N} (r_u + s_{J,u}^Q) \, du \right) \right] \\ &= \exp[(A_R(N) + A_J(N)) + (B_R'(N) + B_J'(N)) X_t] \end{aligned} \tag{2.6}$$

---

[2] Bolder (2001) and Piazzesi (2009) give an overview of the theoretical concepts of affine term structure models.

The risk-free zero coupon yields of government bonds can be expressed as:

$$y_{R,t}(N) = -\frac{\ln P_{R,t}(N)}{N} = -\frac{1}{N}[A_R(N) + B'_R(N)X_t]. \qquad (2.7)$$

Similarly, zero coupon yields of defaultable bonds can be obtained from:

$$y_{J,t}(N) = -\frac{\ln P_{J,t}(N)}{N} = -\frac{1}{N}[(A_R(N) + A_J(N)) + (B'_R(N) + B'_J(N))X_t]. \qquad (2.8)$$

And credit spreads of rating class J and time to maturity N are then defined as:

$$s_{J,t}(N) = y_{R,t}(N) - y_{J,t}(N) = -\frac{1}{N}[A_J(N) + B'_J(N)X_t]. \qquad (2.9)$$

As shown in Equation (2.9), the term structure of credit spreads can directly be derived from functions A_J and B_J. Thus, there is no need to calculate the term structure of defaultable bond yields first. This is because yields are linear functions of the state variables.

Under the local expectation hypothesis (LEH), the bond price Equations (2.5) and (2.6) would also hold under the data generating measure, as the LEH implies that the risk-neutral and the empirical measures coincide. The empirically relevant case, however, is that the LEH does not hold. Consequently, a market price of systematic risk needs to be included that links the data generating measure to the risk-neutral measure.[3] The stochastic part of the process in Equation (2.3) becomes

$$dW_t^* = dW_t - \lambda_t dt. \qquad (2.10)$$

Modeling the market price of risk λ_t as an affine function of the state factors with a constant vector λ_0 and a time-varying matrix λ_1 results in:[4]

$$\lambda_t = \lambda_0 + \lambda_1 X_t. \qquad (2.11)$$

Following Amato and Luisi (2006), all elements in λ_0 are unrestricted, and the matrix λ_1 is restricted according to

---

3   See, e.g., Ang and Piazzesi (2003) for a detailed review of bond pricing under the LEH and without the LEH.
4   See Ang and Piazzesi (2003), Rudebusch *et al.* (2006), Terazzan (2006), or Lemke (2008), among others.

$$\lambda_1 = \begin{pmatrix} \lambda_{1(1,1)} & 0 & 0 & 0 & 0 & 0 \\ 0 & \lambda_{1(2,2)} & 0 & 0 & 0 & 0 \\ 0 & 0 & \lambda_{1(3,3)} & 0 & 0 & 0 \\ 0 & 0 & 0 & \lambda_{1(f,f)} & \lambda_{1(f,y)} & \lambda_{1(f,\pi)} \\ 0 & 0 & 0 & \lambda_{1(y,f)} & \lambda_{1(y,y)} & \lambda_{1(y,\pi)} \\ 0 & 0 & 0 & \lambda_{1(\pi,f)} & \lambda_{1(\pi,y)} & \lambda_{1(\pi,\pi)} \end{pmatrix}, \qquad (2.12)$$

where f, y, and π refer to the observable macro factors financial activity, real activity, and inflation, respectively.

Having defined the general bond pricing formulae in the exponential affine term structure model, the solutions for $A(N)$ and $B(N)$ for risk-free yields and credit spreads in Equations (2.8) and (2.9), respectively, need to be derived. According to Duffie and Kan (1996), functions $A(N)$ and $B(N)$ are obtained as solutions to the ordinary differential equations (ODEs):

$$\begin{aligned} \frac{\partial A_R(N)}{\partial N} &= -\delta_0 + B_R'(N) K^* \overline{X}^* + \frac{1}{2} \sum_{i=1}^M \left[B_R'(N) \Sigma \right]_i^2 \\ \frac{\partial B_R(N)}{\partial N} &= -\delta_1 - K^{*\prime} B_R(N) \end{aligned} \qquad (2.13)$$

Given that the terminal value of a zero coupon bond is equal to 1 (which implies that it pays off its face value at maturity ($N = 0$)), the boundary conditions of $A_R(0) = 0$ and $B_R(0) = 0_{6 \times 1}$ can be imposed on the ODEs in Equation (2.13).

Similarly, for the credit spreads in Equation (2.9), the set of ODEs is:

$$\begin{aligned} \frac{\partial A_J(N)}{\partial N} &= -\gamma_{J,0} + B_J'(N) K^* \overline{X}^* + \frac{1}{2} \sum_{i=1}^M \left[B_J'(N) \Sigma \right]_i^2 \\ \frac{\partial B_J(N)}{\partial N} &= -\gamma_{J,1} - K^{*\prime} B_R(N) \end{aligned} \qquad (2.14)$$

with the boundary conditions $A_J(0) = 0$ and $B_J(0) = 0_{6 \times 1}$.

Note that the mean reversion matrix and the vector of long-term means in Equations (2.13) and (2.14) are expressed under the risk-neutral probability measure, denoted by an asterisk. The link to the data generating measure can be established by relating the risk-neutral forms of the variables to the market price of risk, as follows:

$$\begin{aligned} K^* &= K - \Sigma \lambda_1 \\ K^* \overline{X}^* &= K \overline{X} + \Sigma \lambda_0 \end{aligned} \qquad (2.15)$$

In the model setup, long-term means under the data generating measure are assumed to be zero ($\overline{X} = 0_{6x1}$). The second equation in Equation (2.15) can thus be simplified to:

$$K^* \overline{X}^* = \Sigma \lambda_0. \tag{2.16}$$

Because of the specification of the framework, $A(N)$ and $B(N)$ cannot be solved analytically. According to Ang and Piazzesi (2003), however, numerical solutions using Runge-Kutta methods are fast and efficient. Having derived the necessary formulae in continuous time, the framework can now be translated into a state-space system in discrete time whose parameters can then be estimated with econometric techniques.

2.2.4 State-Space System

According to Bolder (2001), it is necessary for empirical testing to specify a measurement system and a transition system, which together build the state-space formulation of the term structure model, as described above. The measurement equation contains a vector z_t of all observed variables on the left-hand side, i.e. the yields and credit spreads of all different maturities as well as the observable macro variables. The yields and spreads are explained on the right-hand side by the affine functions of the state variables defined in Equations (2.7) and (2.9). In matrix notation, the measurement equation can be expressed as:

$$z_t = a + bX_t + \varepsilon_t, \tag{2.17}$$

where vector a and matrix b contain the solutions for the ODEs for the different yield and spread series, and reflect the time to maturity of the respective yield/spread data. More specifically, the elements of a and b already contain the terms $-A(N)/N$ and $-B(N)/N$ for the respective time to maturity N of the corresponding element in z_t. The last three elements of a are equal to zero in order to allow for the equality of the measurement equation with regard to the observed macro factors. Similarly, the last three row vectors of b are equal to [0 0 0 1 0 0], [0 0 0 0 1 0], and [0 0 0 0 0 1].

According to Amato and Luisi (2006), all yields and spreads are assumed to be measured with errors, so that $\varepsilon_t \sim N(0, R)$. R is a diagonal variance matrix allowing for maturity-dependent variances within the different subsets of yields and spreads. Thus, any serial correlation or cross-correlation in the measurement errors can be prevented, although yields and spreads are nevertheless correlated through the common state variables.

The last three entries of the main diagonal of R are zero, as the error terms for the three observed macro factors are included in the state vector dynamics. The definition of vector a and matrices b and R leads to a perfect update inference of the observed state variables during the Kalman filtering steps.[5]

The transition system must reflect the dynamics of the state process in Equation (2.3). For empirical testing, a discretized version of the state process in Equation (2.3) is required, which can be expressed as:

$$X_t = C + FX_{t-1} + Q\upsilon_t, \qquad (2.18)$$

where $C \equiv \overline{X} - \exp(-Kh)\overline{X}$, $F \equiv \exp(-Kh)$, and h is the time horizon of the discrete process. Because the data contains monthly observations, h is equal to 1/12. According to Bolder (2001) or Amato and Luisi (2006), Equation (2.18) is equivalent to a vector autoregression process of order 1, VAR(1). The error terms of the state process in Equation (2.18) are assumed to be normally distributed with a mean of zero, so that $\upsilon_t \sim N(0, I)$. The unobserved state variables are normalized to have conditional variances of 1, and the upper-left 3×3 matrix of Q is equal to the identity matrix. Because the long-term means of the state factors entering $\overline{X}$ are assumed to be zero, Equation (2.18) can be simplified to:

$$X_t = FX_{t-1} + Q\upsilon_t, \qquad (2.19)$$

as C becomes $0_{6 \times 1}$. Finally, discrete versions of the ODE solutions in Equation (2.13) are used for risk-free yields (see Rudebusch and Wu (2008) and Ang and Piazzesi (2003)):

$$\begin{aligned} A_{R,n+1} &= A_{R,n} + B'_{R,n} F^* \overline{X}^* + \frac{1}{2} B'_{R,n} QQ' B_{R,n} - \delta_0, \\ B_{R,n+1} &= F^{*'} B_{R,n} - \delta_1 \end{aligned} \qquad (2.20)$$

with the initial conditions of $A_{R,0} = 0$ and $B_{R,0} = 0_{6 \times 1}$.

Likewise, from Equation (2.14), the difference equations for credit spreads are specified as

$$\begin{aligned} A_{J,t+1} &= A_{J,t} + B'_{J,t} F^* \overline{X}^* + \frac{1}{2} B'_{J,t} QQ' B_{J,t} - \gamma_{J,0}, \\ B_{J,t+1} &= F^{*'} B_{J,t} - \gamma_{J,1} \end{aligned} \qquad (2.21)$$

with the initial conditions of $A_{J,0} = 0$ and $B_{J,0} = 0_{6 \times 1}$.

---

5 See also Dewachter and Lyrio (2006) for a description of the Kalman filter mechanisms when observed variables are included in the state dynamics.

The risk-neutral terms entering the difference equations are similarly defined as in continuous time, only with the variables of the discrete version of the state process:

$$F^* = F - Q\lambda_1$$
$$F^*\overline{X}^* = C - Q\lambda_0$$
(2.22)

2.3 Data

In order to estimate the macro-finance term structure model of credit spreads for the euro zone, three different data sources and methodologies are required. In the following sections, 1) the time series of risk-free yields, 2) the yields of defaultable bonds and the resulting credit spreads, and 3) the macro factors are discussed in turn.

2.3.1 Risk-free Yields

Several papers on European term structure models use different time series to represent the risk-free yields over time.[6] To ensure a geographically consistent data set of risk-free yields that is aligned with the data of defaultable bond yields and macro variables (both observed in the EU), Bloomberg data on the fair market curve of AAA EU government bonds is used.

The data range from January 2000 through September 2008, with maturities of three and six months, as well as one, two, three, four, five, seven, eight, nine, and ten years. Because the data reflect the par yield curve, the method of Nelson and Siegel (1987) is used to convert the yields to zero coupons at the different monthly observation points.

Table 2-1 provides the descriptive statistics for the risk-free zero coupon yields. The standard assumption of a normal yield curve with yields that increase with time to maturity is supported by the means of the annualized zero coupon rates.

---

6   Terazzan (2006) uses the benchmark government bond yield series published by the European Central Bank. Lemke (2008) applies yields of German government bonds for pre-1999 data, and Bloomberg zero coupon swap rates for post-1999 data. Van Landschoot (2004) uses AAA-rated government bonds that are included in the *EMU Government Broad Market* index.

Table 2-1: Summary statistics of risk-free yields

Time to maturity (years)	Mean	Standard Deviation	Skewness	Kurtosis	Min	Max	Autocorrelation			
							Lag 1	Lag 2	Lag 3	Lag 4
0.25	3.21	0.97	0.09	1.67	1.86	5.07	0.98	0.95	0.92	0.88
0.5	3.25	0.96	0.10	1.69	1.86	5.07	0.98	0.95	0.91	0.87
1	3.33	0.94	0.09	1.75	1.92	5.19	0.97	0.94	0.89	0.85
2	3.48	0.87	0.10	1.85	2.03	5.27	0.96	0.91	0.85	0.80
3	3.64	0.81	0.13	1.96	2.18	5.29	0.95	0.88	0.83	0.76
4	3.78	0.75	0.16	2.07	2.35	5.31	0.94	0.87	0.81	0.74
5	3.91	0.70	0.19	2.17	2.52	5.31	0.94	0.86	0.80	0.74
7	4.12	0.64	0.18	2.28	2.83	5.40	0.94	0.86	0.81	0.75
8	4.20	0.62	0.15	2.29	2.95	5.46	0.94	0.87	0.82	0.76
9	4.28	0.61	0.11	2.27	3.05	5.50	0.94	0.87	0.82	0.77
10	4.34	0.60	0.07	2.25	3.13	5.54	0.94	0.87	0.83	0.78

This table reports the statistics for risk-free yields of different maturities included in the sample. The values for mean, standard deviation, minimum, and maximum are shown as annualized percentage rates. The data sample includes 105 data points of monthly observations from January 2000 through September 2008.

Figure 2-1 depicts the time series of the zero coupon risk-free yields for three months and for two, five, and ten years. Note that the shape of the yield curve changes substantially during the sample period. After a long period of a relatively steep yield curve from 2001 to mid-2006, it becomes very flat from mid-2006 through the end of 2008. This indicates that investors were quite risk-averse toward holding long-term bonds in the first period, and became almost risk-neutral during more recent times. To estimate the model parameters, zero coupon yields with maturities of three months, six months, and one, three, five, and ten years are used.

Figure 2-1: Risk-free zero coupon yields

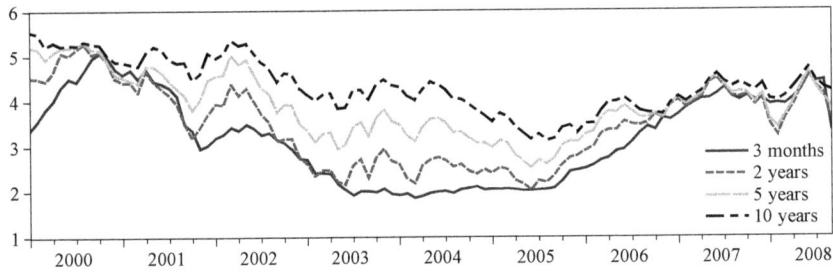

This figure shows the time series for selected maturities of zero coupon risk-free yields during the sample period of January 2000-September 2008. Yields are shown as annualized percentage rates.

2.3.2 Credit Spreads

To obtain a term structure of credit spreads for different credit ratings, first a sufficiently long time series of data on European defaultable bonds with different times to maturity categorized in distinct credit classes is required. To establish this, a database is constructed that consists of corporate bonds listed in the *iBoxx Corporate Index* of euro-denominated bonds.[7]

In order to build a pure European term structure model, any bonds issued by non-EU companies are excluded. Subsequently the bonds are categorized into the credit rating classes AA, A, and BBB that are published in the iBoxx index. Because of the limited availability of bond data in some credit rating classes before 2000, and the requirement that the data span the complete time horizon of maturities, the sample period is January 2000 through September 2008.

Table 2-2 summarizes the sample statistics of the corporate bond database. Note that the subsample of A-rated bonds contains the most observations. Those results are expected to be the most robust.

---

[7] The corporate bond sample contains a total of 1,233 bonds from 18 different industry sectors (defined by iBoxx as Sector Level 4). An overview of the industry mix in the sample is available upon request.

Table 2-2: Summary statistics of corporate credit spreads

Time to maturity (years)	Mean	Standard Deviation	Skewness	Kurtosis	Min	Max	Autocorrelation			
							Lag 1	Lag 2	Lag 3	Lag 4
AA-rated credit spreads										
1	26	28	2.84	13.29	-35	182	0.73	0.67	0.61	0.54
2	27	28	3.33	15.51	-7	194	0.76	0.68	0.62	0.55
3	32	32	2.91	11.17	9	192	0.85	0.76	0.68	0.59
4	36	31	2.90	12.72	10	210	0.80	0.72	0.66	0.57
5	42	37	3.06	14.35	12	255	0.78	0.69	0.63	0.55
7	57	52	2.64	9.51	17	291	0.87	0.78	0.70	0.62
8	58	40	2.38	9.85	20	261	0.82	0.75	0.68	0.60
9	60	37	2.41	11.82	23	269	0.78	0.69	0.63	0.57
10	66	44	2.39	10.29	26	296	0.82	0.72	0.64	0.57
A-rated credit spreads										
1	53	40	2.83	11.29	9	242	0.84	0.73	0.60	0.48
2	53	34	2.71	12.49	18	242	0.80	0.71	0.62	0.54
3	60	40	1.99	7.99	20	253	0.84	0.77	0.70	0.63
4	65	39	1.96	8.49	23	265	0.81	0.75	0.69	0.62
5	72	42	2.04	8.87	28	286	0.83	0.75	0.66	0.58
7	90	65	2.52	10.81	30	433	0.82	0.74	0.66	0.60
8	102	77	2.86	12.28	39	524	0.81	0.74	0.66	0.60
9	105	65	2.64	10.36	44	435	0.84	0.76	0.69	0.63
10	97	38	1.72	6.11	42	257	0.86	0.79	0.71	0.65
BBB-rated credit spreads										
1	74	50	1.37	4.32	10	234	0.82	0.71	0.62	0.57
2	89	56	0.80	2.37	27	226	0.90	0.83	0.78	0.75
3	104	66	1.06	3.71	30	325	0.88	0.79	0.72	0.67
4	113	67	0.91	3.13	39	321	0.90	0.82	0.76	0.70
5	108	51	1.02	3.77	44	300	0.88	0.81	0.75	0.68
7	134	68	1.05	3.96	53	400	0.87	0.79	0.71	0.66
8	158	74	0.66	2.47	53	388	0.89	0.79	0.69	0.65
9	157	64	0.43	2.27	55	324	0.88	0.77	0.69	0.65
10	171	88	0.92	3.17	58	429	0.88	0.75	0.68	0.65

This table reports the statistics for credit spreads of different maturities included in the sample. Values for mean, standard deviation, minimum, and maximum are shown as basis points. The data sample includes 105 data points of monthly observations from January 2000 through September 2008 for each panel (AA, A, and BBB credit spreads). The total number of observations for AA credit spreads is 8,979, with a minimum, maximum, and average coupon rate of 0.0, 9.8, and 4.7, respectively. For A, there are 23,537 observations, with a minimum, maximum, and average coupon rate of 2.0, 10.0, and 5.1, respectively. For BBB, there are 14,222 observations, with a minimum, maximum, and average coupon rate of 3.0, 8.1, and 5.4, respectively. Overall, there are 46,738 observations, with a minimum, maximum, and average coupon rate of 0.0, 10.0, and 5.1.

To derive zero coupon yield curves for each rating category at every monthly observation point an approach similar to Terazzan (2006) is used. First the annual yields to maturity for each bond are calculated based on settlement date, closing price, time to maturity, annual coupon rate, number of coupon payments per year, and day count basis. Then a bootstrapping technique is applied to convert the yields to maturity into zero coupon yields for every point where a cash flow payment is due. Based on these intermediate results, a cubic spline is fitted for all the data, so that a smoothed zero coupon yield curve is obtained for the one-, two-, three-, four-, five-, seven-, eight-, nine-, and ten-year maturities. Finally, AA, A, and BBB credit spreads are derived by subtracting risk-free zero coupon yields from the respective zero coupon corporate bond yields with the same time to maturity.

As expected, two major observations are noted about the credit spreads. First, for all rating categories, the average credit spread curves are upward-sloping. The only exceptions are the ten-year A credit spread, which is on average smaller than the eight- and nine-year spreads, and the five-year BBB credit spread, which is below the four- and seven-year BBB credit spreads. Second, average AA credit spreads are smaller than average A credit spreads at all maturities, which in turn are smaller than average BBB credit spreads. Figure 2-2 depicts these characteristics.

Figure 2-2: Mean credit spread curves

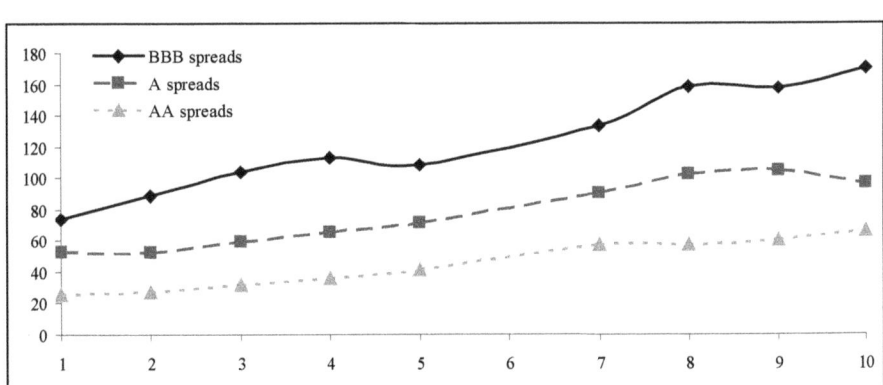

This figure shows the average credit spreads for the AA, A, and BBB corporate bonds in the sample. The x-axis shows the time to maturity of the corresponding zero coupon bond; the y-axis shows the average credit spread in basis points.

41

Figure 2-3 shows the credit spreads for AA, A, and BBB corporate bonds in the sample for the one-, two-, five-, and ten-year maturities. Note that the credit spread curves are not always upward-sloping during the time horizon. There are data points where bonds with longer times to maturity exhibit smaller credit spreads than those with shorter times to maturity. This illustrates that sometimes the risk premium associated with holding bonds with longer times to maturity is negative.

Figure 2-3: Credit spreads of corporate bonds

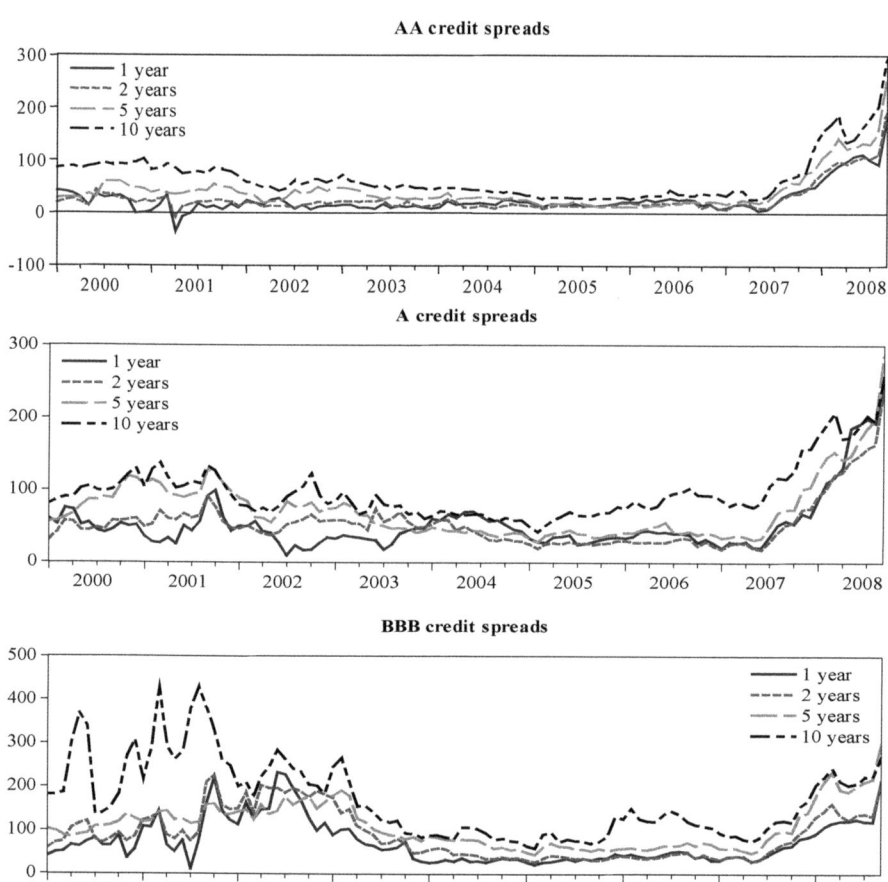

This figure shows the credit spreads in basis points calculated as the difference between the annualized zero coupon yields of corporate bonds and risk-free bonds with the corresponding time to maturity.

For example, consider the rating category A between Q1 and Q4 2004, where the one-year spread is significantly larger than the two- and five-year spreads, and approximately on the same level as the ten-year spread. One challenge of the term structure model is to explain these inverse credit spread curves, because they indicate that the risk premiums are not constant but vary by time. To estimate the model parameters, credit spreads with one-, three-, five-, seven-, and nine-year maturities are used.

2.3.3 Macroeconomic Variables

Following the methods of Ang and Piazzesi (2003) and Amato and Luisi (2006), this study includes three macro variables as observable state factors in the term structure model: inflation, real activity, and financial activity. All three factors are constructed from more fundamental variables using principal component analysis (PCA).

For the inflation factor, three different price indices published by the European Central Bank (ECB) are included: the *harmonized consumer price index* (CPI), the *producer price index excluding construction and energy related companies* (PPI), and the *producer price index for energy related companies* (ENERGY). The inflation factor time series is constructed from the twelve-month log differences of end-of-month observations of the indices.

The macro factor for real activity is built from four different data series published by the ECB: the *growth rate of employment* (EMPLOY), the *unemployment rate* (UNEMPLOY), the *growth rate of the industrial producer index* (PRODUCTION), and the *growth rate of the new orders index* (ORDERS). Growth rates are again calculated as twelve-month log differences of the respective data series. Data for EMPLOY, UNEMPLOY, and PRODUCTION are reported on a monthly basis, and are thus entered as end-of-month observations. The EMPLOY variable is only quarterly, so the technique of Fernández (1981) is used to interpolate the monthly data points.

The unknown monthly values of EMPLOY are assumed to be linear combinations of the known monthly values of the other three variables. Under the restriction that the averages of the interpolated monthly data points equal the observed quarterly values of EMPLOY, monthly data points are constructed that "minimize a quadratic loss function in the differences between the series to be created and a linear combination of the high frequency series" (Fernández (1981, p. 471)).

Figure 2-4: Macroeconomic factors

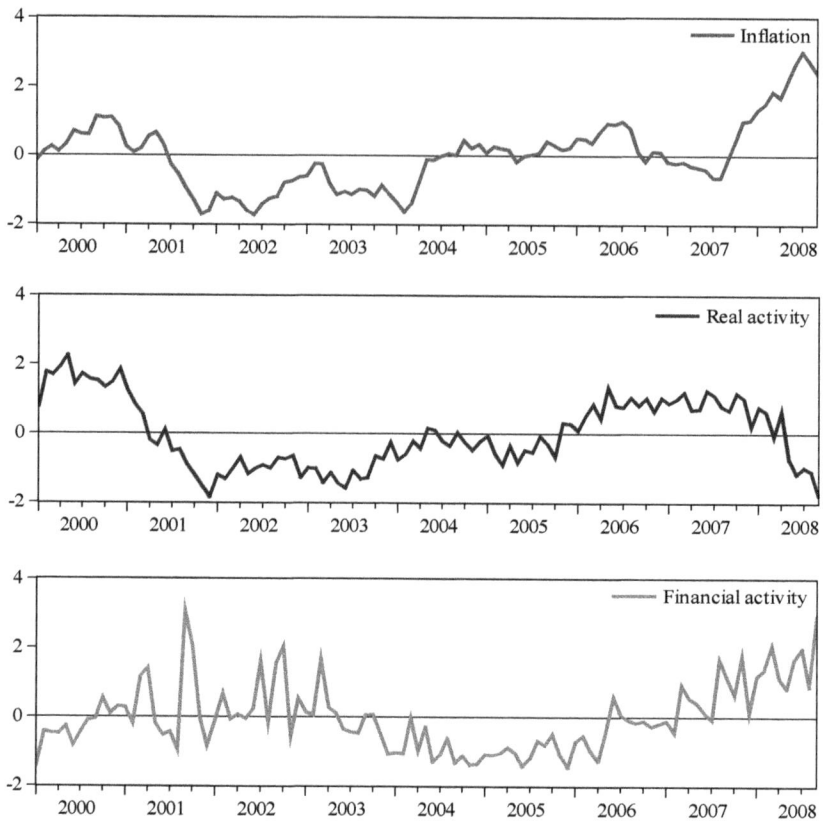

This figure shows the macro factors constructed from the variables CPI, PPI, and ENERGY for the inflation factor, EMPLOY, UNEMPLOY, PRODUCTION, and ORDERS for real activity, and LEVERAGE, INTCOV, CASHFLOW, and VOLA for financial activity. The macro factors depicted are the first principal components of the respective group of variables. They are normalized to have means of zero and unit variances.

Following Amato and Luisi (2006), the financial activity factor is constructed using: 1) a leverage ratio (LEVERAGE), calculated by dividing the *European institutional sector debt* by the *four-quarter operating surplus*, 2) the interest coverage ratio (INTCOV), calculated by dividing *interest payments of the European institutional sector* by the *nominal gross domestic product*, and 3) a cash flow proxy (CASHFLOW), calculated as the *four-quarter operating surplus of the European institutional sector* divided by the *four-quarter final sales of domestic product*.

Because data for the latter are not directly available from the ECB statistical database, the data are derived by subtracting the *four-quarter change in inventory* from the *four-quarter nominal gross domestic product*. For all data, quarterly time series from the ECB that include only non-financial corporations are used.

Finally, a monthly time series for volatility (VOLA) is constructed by using the monthly averages of the daily implied volatility figures of the *DJ EuroStoxx 50 Index* published by Thomson Reuters Datastream. Again, the monthly time series of VOLA is used to interpolate the quarterly time series of LEVERAGE, INTCOV, and CASHFLOW to monthly data. Figure 2-4 plots the three macro factors that are in the macro-finance model.

To construct the macro factors from the monthly time series, first the individual variables are normalized. Then the first principal components extracted from the three groups of macroeconomic variables that belong to inflation, real activity, and financial activity, which capture 63%, 64%, and 36%, respectively, of the total variance are used.[8]

Because macroeconomic data are used for ordinary least squares (OLS) estimates, non-stationarity of the time series is a potential issue. Therefore, Augmented Dickey-Fuller (ADF) tests are performed on the constructed macro factors.[9] Except for the inflation factor time series, ADF test statistics reject the null of a unit root at conventional levels of significance.[10]

In order to test for stability of the VAR(1) process in Equation (2.19), the roots of the characteristic autoregressive polynomial according to Lütkepohl (1991) are calculated. All eigenvalues of the coefficient matrix have modulus of less than 1.[11] So the estimated VAR can be considered stable and the parameter estimates presented in section 2.4 can be used for further estimation.

2.4 Research Strategy and Estimation Results

The parameters of the term structure model are estimated using the two-step approach of Ang and Piazzesi (2003). First, a subset of parameters is derived using OLS. Then these parameters are used as input variables to estimate the remaining model parameters with the maximum likelihood (ML) technique.

---

8   The results of the PCA for the three macro factors are available upon request.
9   The results of the ADF unit root tests are available upon request.
10 Other authors have confirmed the evidence of non-stationary time series of inflation. See, e.g., Banerjee and Russell (2001), and Russell and Banerjee (2008).
11 This means that the characteristic polynomial has no roots in and on the complex unit circle.

The macro factors are not assumed to interact with the risk-free yields and corporate spreads, but are exogenous to the system. Thus, the parameters of the short rate processes defined in Equations (2.1) and (2.2) that are related to the observed macro variables can be estimated by OLS. The parameters of δ_1 ($\gamma_{J,1}$) that refer to the observed macro factors can be estimated by regressing the instantaneous risk-free yield (instantaneous credit spread) on the inflation, real activity, and financial activity factors. The three-month zero coupon yield and the three credit spread series with a one-year time to maturity are used to approximate the instantaneous risk-free rate and the instantaneous credit spreads, respectively.

According to Ang and Piazzesi (2003), the constants δ_0 and $\gamma_{J,0}$ can be set to the unconditional means of the short rates for risk-free yields and credit spreads, respectively. This is because the macro factors are constructed to have means of zero. The unconditional means of the three-month risk-free yield and the one-year credit spreads for the AA, A, and BBB rating categories are all expressed as annualized rates. Hence, the respective unconditional means need to be divided by 12, so that δ_0 and $\gamma_{J,0}$ reflect the constants of the short rate at a monthly frequency, corresponding to the setup of the discrete state-space model with monthly observations.

The second set of OLS estimates consists of the parameters of the state dynamics related to the observable macro factors. Specifically, these are the elements of the mean reversion matrix K in Equation (2.4) that refer to the factors inflation, real activity, and financial activity. In this case, these elements are in the lower-right 3 × 3 matrix of K. As described above, the VAR(1) process from Equation (2.18) reflects a discretized version of the state dynamics, so that only the elements of the transformed matrix F can be tested empirically.

Having estimated δ_1, $\gamma_{J,1}$, and certain elements of F by using OLS, and having used unconditional means for δ_0 and $\gamma_{J,0}$, next the remaining parameters of the term structure model are estimated using maximum likelihood and holding the OLS estimates fixed. In line with standard term structure literature, the likelihood function is constructed by applying a Kalman filtering technique.[12] The smooth and non-linear log-likelihood function is maximized to find the optimal parameter vector by using a non-linear numerical optimization technique and applying a BFGS Quasi-Newton method.[13] Asymptotic standard errors for the ML estimates are calculated numerically as square roots of the inverse of the Hessian (as shown, for example, in Bolder (2001)). The OLS parameters are assumed to be estimated without error in step one.

---

12 A theoretical derivation of the formulae used for the Kalman filter can be found in, e.g., Merkus et al. (1993), Bolder (2001), and Date and Wang (2009).
13 See Broyden (1970), Fletcher (1970), Goldfarb (1970), and Shanno (1970).

Table 2-3: Parameter estimates of the term structure model

VARIABLE	INDEX	0	1	2	3	f	y	π
Short-rate parameters								
δ	i	0.268	0.021 (0.001) *	0.001 (0.000)	-0.003 (0.000) *	0.042 (0.006) *	0.040 (0.006) *	0.012 (0.006) *
γ_{AA}	i	0.021	-0.008 (0.001) *	-0.002 (0.000) *	-0.004 (0.000) *	0.004 (0.001) *	-0.005 (0.002) *	0.014 (0.002) *
γ_A	i	0.044	-0.009 (0.001) *	-0.001 (0.000) *	-0.005 (0.000) *	0.007 (0.002) *	-0.011 (0.002) *	0.021 (0.002) *
γ_{BBB}	i	0.061	-0.010 (0.001) *	0.009 (0.000) *	-0.003 (0.000) *	0.026 (0.003) *	-0.011 (0.003) *	-0.007 (0.003) *
Mean reversion speed matrix (discrete time)								
F	$1,i$	-	0.960 (0.004) *	0	0	0	0	0
F	$2,i$	-	0.006 (0.002) *	0.952 (0.003) *	0	0	0	0
F	$3,i$	-	0.030 (0.002) *	-0.007 (0.000) *	0.997 (0.003) *	0	0	0
F	f,i	-	0	0	0	0.589 (0.084) *	-0.023 (0.089)	0.123 (0.091)
F	y,i	-	0	0	0	-0.088 (0.044) *	0.920 (0.046) *	-0.016 (0.047)
F	π,i	-	0	0	0	0.002 (0.030)	-0.023 (0.032)	0.971 (0.033) *
Market price of risk								
λ_0	i	-	1.904 (0.013) *	-5.311 (0.038) *	-2.509 (0.018) *	1.617 (0.018) *	-4.308 (0.021) *	-4.356 (0.016) *
λ_1	$1,i$	-	-0.021 (0.004) *	0	0	0	0	0
λ_1	$2,i$	-	0	-0.044 (0.004) *	0	0	0	0
λ_1	$3,i$	-	0	0	-0.011 (0.003) *	0	0	0
λ_1	f,i	-	0	0	0	1.017 (0.028) *	0.451 (0.011) *	0.623 (0.005) *
λ_1	y,i	-	0	0	0	0.920 (0.023) *	0.159 (0.008) *	0.350 (0.004) *
λ_1	π,i	-	0	0	0	0.589 (0.014) *	0.097 (0.005) *	0.102 (0.004) *
Volatility of measurement errors								
$(R/N)_{IE}$		0.004 (0.000) *						
$(R/N)_{AA}$		0.001 (0.000) *						
$(R/N)_A$		0.002 (0.000) *						
$(R/N)_{BBB}$		0.003 (0.000) *						

*This table shows the parameter estimates of the term structure model. Asymptotic standard errors for the ML estimates are calculated numerically as square roots of the inverse Hessian (see Bolder (2001)), and are reported in brackets. * denotes significant parameters at a 5% significance level. Parameters in the bordered areas (25 in total) are estimated by OLS; the remaining parameters (40 in total) are estimated by ML. The log-likelihood function has a value of 5,899.*

Note from Table 2-3 that the first set of parameters estimated by OLS consists of the loadings on the observable macro factors in the instantaneous risk-free rate (the last three elements of δ_1), and the instantaneous credit spreads (the last three elements of $\gamma_{J,1}$). These are defined in Equations (2.1) and (2.2), respectively.

As described above, the three-month risk-free yields and the one-year credit spreads are regressed on the inflation, real activity, and financial activity factors. The estimates for the risk-free yield show a positive relationship between all observable macro factors and the instantaneous interest rate. This implies that monetary policy reacts with increasing interest rates to positive shocks to inflation, real activity, and financial activity.

This result confirms standard macroeconomic theory that central banks increase the short end of the yield curve when macro factors indicate an overheating economy. The results are in line with the findings of Amato and Luisi (2006) and Ang and Piazzesi (2003), who also confirm positive relationships between their respective macro variables and the short-term risk-free rate. Furthermore, it can be inferred that shocks to financial activity ($\delta_f = 0.042$) and real activity ($\delta_y = 0.040$) have a stronger impact on the short rate than inflation ($\delta_\pi = 0.012$), as the macro factors are all normalized.

The regressions of the three credit spread time series show a positive impact of shocks to the financial activity factor on the instantaneous credit spreads. This indicates a widening of spreads in response to the increasing risk that is associated with the rising leverage of companies. In contrast to the risk-free short rate, the instantaneous credit spreads of all rating categories decrease with positive shocks to real activity. This result can be explained by the fact that the default risk across all companies, which is expressed by the credit spread, decreases during times of economic upturns, and increases during economic downturns. The findings for financial activity and real activity are comparable to those of Amato and Luisi (2006).

The impact of increasing inflation on the instantaneous credit spreads is different for the AA and A rating classes than it is for the BBB class. Although instantaneous credit spreads of AA or A companies widen with positive inflation shocks, those of BBB companies seem to tighten slightly. The estimates of the loadings on the inflation factor for AA and A spreads again confirm the findings of Amato and Luisi (2006); the estimate of the loading for BBB spreads does not.

As discussed later, this differing behavior of BBB spreads can be traced throughout the model and is also reflected by the structure of the latent factors. In terms of the absolute size of the impact on instantaneous credit spreads, inflation has the biggest impact on spreads of AA-rated corporate bonds ($\gamma_{AA,\pi} =$

0.014) and A-rated bonds ($\gamma_{A,\pi} = 0.021$). Financial activity has the largest impact on BBB-rated bonds ($\gamma_{BBB,f} = 0.026$).

The second set of parameters estimated by OLS consists of the elements of the mean reversion matrix in the state dynamics defined in Equation (2.4) that refer to the observed macro factors. Using the discrete version of the state dynamics in Equation (2.19), the lower-right 3 × 3 matrix of F can thus be estimated.

The estimated parameters show high persistence for real activity ($F_{y,y} = 0.920$) and inflation ($F_{\pi,\pi} = 0.971$), and less persistence for financial activity ($F_{f,f} = 0.589$). Compared to the VAR coefficients estimated by Amato and Luisi (2006), the autoregression coefficient for financial activity is much less persistent, but those for inflation and real activity are comparable. Only one coefficient in the estimated VAR model that specifies cross-correlation between level and lagged macro factors is found to be significant, $F_{y,f} = -0.088$, which indicates a low negative relationship between real activity and lagged financial activity.

Turning to the ML estimates, first the remaining parameters of the short rate equations for risk-free yields and credit spreads are discussed. The estimates for the loadings on the three latent factors in the instantaneous risk-free rate and the instantaneous credit spreads are all significant at the 5% level, except for δ_2. The loadings on the third latent factor (Latent 3) are negative for the risk-free rate and for the instantaneous credit spreads of all rating categories. But those on the first two latent factors (Latents 1 and 2) have mixed signs.

Second, the remaining parameters of the mean reversion matrix F in discrete time for the latent factors reflect a high persistence for all three factors, with Latent 3 showing the strongest autocorrelation. In contrast to the macro factors, the cross-correlation coefficients are also significant, which indicates an existing interaction between the latent factors. These findings are again in line with Amato and Luisi (2006), who find a relatively high persistence of all latent factors, although their third latent factor is less autocorrelated than the other two.

Third, the estimates of the market price of systematic risk for the six factors are discussed. As noted above, the model setup differentiates between the time-independent (vector λ_0) and the time-dependent (matrix λ_1) market price of risk. All estimated parameters of λ_0 and λ_1 are significant, which implies that all factors contribute to the systematic risk premiums inherent in bond prices.

Note that the elements of λ_0 for Latent 1 and the financial activity factor have positive signs, while the elements for all other individual factors have negative signs. Negative signs in λ_0 imply that the unconditional mean of the short rate is higher under the risk-neutral measure than under the data generating measure. The estimates thus support the hypothesis that yields and credit spreads with longer times to maturity are on average higher than those with shorter times to maturity. This indicates that the risk factors explain the observed upward-sloping yield and spread curves, because the four negative elements of λ_0 outweigh the positive parameters for Latent 1 and for financial activity.

However, the results are slightly different than those of Amato and Luisi (2006), who find significant negative estimates for all six factors. A plausible interpretation for the fact that not all six time-independent components of the market price of risk have negative signs is that the risk factors do not contribute uniformly to the observed term structures of yields and credit spreads. Instead, Latent 1 and financial activity act as counterbalances to the other risk factors, because they imply downward-sloping average yield and spread curves.

One reason for this effect could be that the credit spread curves used in this model do not follow the law of one price and the absence of arbitrage opportunities in a completely stringent way. As discussed earlier, this is considered as confirmation of the assumption that financial integration in the European bond market has not yet reached U.S. levels.

For the time variation in the market price of systematic risk, which is reflected in λ_1, the results of this study are more differentiated. Note that the parameters of the latent factors have negative signs. According to Amato and Luisi (2006), this causes the risk premiums and credit spreads to increase more strongly for longer maturities after positive shocks to those factors. The macro factors, on the other hand, all have positive signs, with the opposite effect on risk premiums and credit spreads. However, given the relative size of the λ_1 elements compared to those of λ_0, the impact of the former on the overall market price of risk is rather small.[14]

Hence, it is concluded that the overall market price of risk is driven mainly by the time-independent part, and any shifts of the yield and spread curves caused by shocks to the (macroeconomic) state factors are generally parallel shifts.[15]

In this regard, the results differ from those of Amato and Luisi (2006), who find negative time-dependent components of the market price of risk for all six risk factors. Their estimates of λ_1 are similar in size to the estimates of λ_0, so their model exhibits a significant time variation for the overall market price of risk.

One reason for these deviations could be that the time horizon of the sample of this study also includes the beginning of the global financial crisis, where an immense widening of credit spreads is observed at all rating categories and over

---

14 This can be illustrated by considering the formula of the market price of risk in Equation (2.11) and the assumption that the long-run means of the state variables are equal to zero.
15 Note that shifts in the yield and spread curves are expressed by the loadings of B in Equations (2.20) and (2.21). However, only λ_1 enters B, so the loadings of λ_1 determine how shocks to the state variables affect yields and spreads of different maturities. In contrast, λ_0 enters A, and thus determines the average shape of the yield and spread curves.

the entire maturity spectrum.[16] Amato and Luisi's (2006) sample, in contrast, is characterized by relatively low volatility. Furthermore, credit spread changes in their sample were not characterized as much by parallel shifts of the spread curve as in the sample period of this study.

2.4.1 Interpretation of Latent Factors

The levels, slopes, and curvatures of the risk-free yields and the credit spreads can be regressed on the filtered time series of the three latent factors. This allows the interpretation of the latent factors as drivers of the observed yield and credit spread curve dynamics.

Following Amato and Luisi (2006), the level of the curves is defined as $(Z_{short} + Z_{med} + Z_{long})/3$, the slope as $Z_{long} - Z_{short}$, and the curvature as $Z_{short} + Z_{long} - 2Z_{med}$, where Z is the yield and credit spread time series of different times to maturity. For the risk-free yields, Z_{short}, Z_{med}, and Z_{long} are equal to the series with times to maturity of three months, three years, and nine years, respectively. The corresponding maturities for credit spreads are one, five, and nine years.

Table 2-4 summarizes the results of the individual univariate regressions of the curve dynamics on the latent factors. Note that Latent 1 is strongly related to the level of the risk-free yield and also explains a substantial part of the slope of the risk-free yield. It has relatively little explanatory power for the credit spread curves. This is again in line with Amato and Luisi (2006), who find that this factor captures much of the persistence of the risk-free yield, because the definition of the short rate does not take into account lagged terms.

Deviations in the credit spread curves are explained more fully by Latents 2 and 3. Latent 2 has the strongest explanatory power for the level of the BBB spreads, but explains less than Latent 3 for the better rated AA and A credit spreads. Latent 3 explains much of the levels and slopes of all the credit spread curves. Thus, this factor is assumed to capture some systematic macroeconomic shocks that are not included in the observable macro variables entering the model. Decreasing market liquidity at the beginning of the financial crisis may explain such a systematic shock that affects credit spreads of all rating categories.

---

16 Zivot and Andrews (1992) unit root tests of the credit spread time series indicate a structural break in the intercept and trend between April and June 2007, which coincides with the beginning of the subprime crisis. Results are available upon request.

Table 2-4: Regression of latent factors on dynamics of yield and spread curves

	Latent 1			Latent 2			Latent 3		
	Est.	Std. err.	R^2	Est.	Std. err.	R^2	Est.	Std. err.	R^2
Risk-free yields									
Level	0.28	0.01	0.82	0.15	0.01	0.54	-0.10	0.01	0.68
Slope	-0.21	0.02	0.46	-0.10	0.02	0.23	0.06	0.01	0.32
Curvature	-0.02	0.02	0.01	0.01	0.01	0.01	0.00	0.01	0.00
AA spreads									
Level	0.05	0.01	0.14	0.04	0.01	0.23	-0.04	0.00	0.58
Slope	0.06	0.01	0.34	0.04	0.00	0.44	-0.02	0.00	0.38
Curvature	-0.02	0.01	0.03	-0.01	0.01	0.04	0.01	0.00	0.13
A spreads									
Level	0.09	0.02	0.20	0.07	0.01	0.27	-0.06	0.00	0.62
Slope	0.09	0.01	0.29	0.06	0.01	0.32	-0.04	0.00	0.51
Curvature	-0.04	0.02	0.03	-0.04	0.01	0.12	-0.01	0.01	0.01
BBB spreads									
Level	0.12	0.02	0.31	0.12	0.01	0.73	-0.06	0.00	0.63
Slope	0.10	0.02	0.26	0.05	0.01	0.19	-0.03	0.01	0.21
Curvature	0.06	0.02	0.07	0.06	0.01	0.15	-0.01	0.01	0.01

This table shows the OLS regression of the dynamics of the observed risk-free yield and credit spread curves on the three filtered latent factors.

Finally, note that overall there seems to be a relatively weak link between the latent factors and the curvature of the yield and spread curves. This implies that common factors can only explain level and steepness and not much of the exact shapes of the yield and spread curves. One reason for this may be the residual segmentation of the European bond market, which may partially violate the law of one price and cause unsmoothed yield and credit spread curves.

2.4.2 Impulse Responses from Shocks to State Factors

In the literature, there are two primary types of impulse responses that are analyzed for the various term structure models. Ang and Piazzesi (2003) and Amato and Luisi (2006) estimate the initial response, i.e., the immediate response at time t of shocks to the state factors on the complete yield or spread curve. The long-term effects of the shock however, i.e., the ongoing effects at times $t + n$, are not considered.

Hördahl et al. (2006), Lemke (2008), and Rudebusch and Wu (2008) present a different approach. They determine the impulse responses of shocks to state factors with regard to yields of selected maturities over a certain time span. They thus identify not only the short-term effects of shocks in the system, but also the long-term effects. The results of both methods are discussed further in this section.

The immediate responses of shocks to the six state factors on the entire yield and spread curves are presented in Figure 2-5. They are derived from the factor loadings B/N as defined in the affine expressions for risk-free yields and credit spreads in Equations (2.7) and (2.9). Overall, Latents 1 and 2, as well as real activity, have a positive impact on risk-free yields. This implies that positive shocks to those factors increase risk-free yields of all maturities.

Note that shocks to Latent 1 have the largest positive impact on short-term risk-free yields, while shocks to real activity affect mid- to long-term risk-free yields with times to maturity of more than sixty months more strongly. Inflation and financial activity both have a positive impact on risk-free yields with very short maturities, but the sign switches for longer maturities, so that both inversely affect the yield curve. Real activity has the largest positive impact and inflation and Latent 3 have the largest negative impact on long-term yields, as the absolute impact of the other three factors is close to zero for long maturities.

Although Amato and Luisi (2006) identify a positive impact of shocks to inflation, with size increasing for longer maturities, in this study a downward-sloping impulse response for that factor is found, with a negative impact on yields with longer maturities. Additionally, the relative importance of the financial factor for risk-free yields is much less than in Amato and Luisi (2006). However, the sign of the impulse responses is the same.

The responses of AA and A spreads to deviations in the state factors are very similar, while BBB spreads react differently. For AA and A spreads, positive shocks to inflation result in almost parallel shifts of the spread curves by approximately 16 and 25 basis points, respectively. This implies that AA and A spreads along the entire spread curve will widen with increasing inflation.

Similarly, shocks to real activity lead to almost parallel downward shifts of the AA and A spread curves. These findings are consistent with the hypothesis that default risk and hence credit spreads increase during market downturns, and that the effect is larger for lower credit ratings.

Figure 2-5: Factor loadings on yields and credit spreads

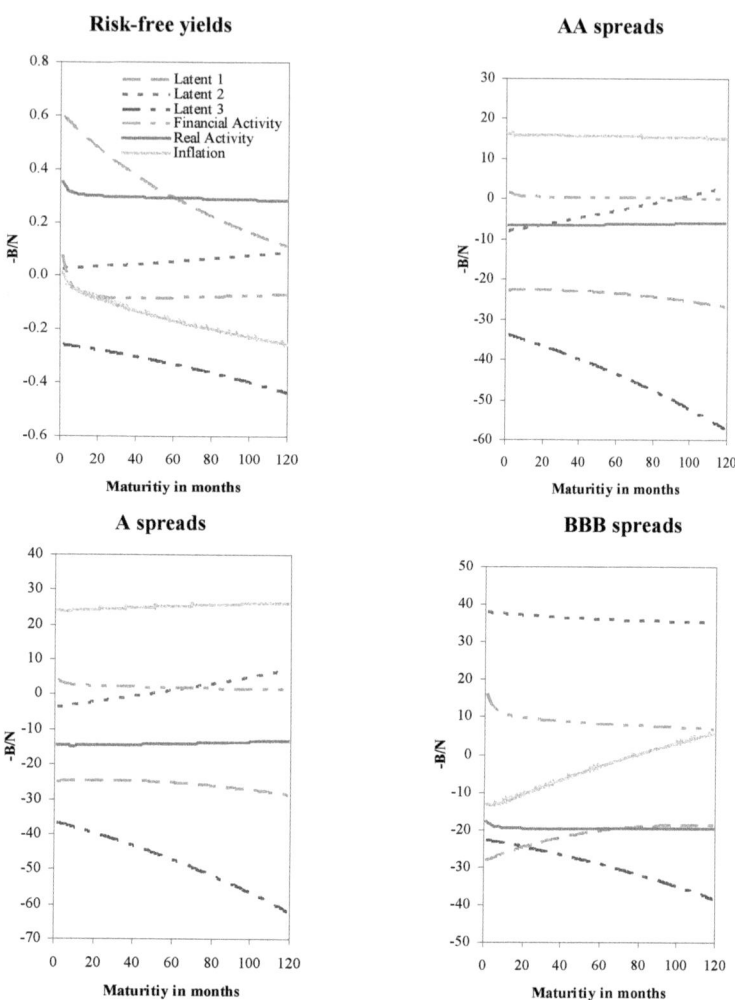

These figures show the estimated immediate response of shocks to the state factors, expressed by the factor loadings –B/N as defined in the affine expressions for risk-free yields and credit spreads in Equations (2.7) and (2.9) respectively. The loadings are scaled to reflect the response of a one-standard deviation shock to the factor. Responses for yields are shown as annualized percentage rates; responses for spreads are shown as annualized basis points.

As discussed above, the shape of the impulse responses is linked to the estimates of the time-dependent market prices of risk. In line with the relatively small values of the elements in the λ_1 matrix, the impulse responses are nearly unchanging with regard to maturity. Thus, the deviations in the B/N factor loadings when compared to Amato and Luisi's (2006) estimates have the same explanation found previously: High volatility in yields and credit spreads with equally strong systematic shocks at all maturities leads to almost parallel shifts of yield and spread curves.

This effect has been driven mainly by the systematic widening of credit spreads since the beginning of the financial crisis. For AA and A ratings, shocks to financial activity have a very small effect. The results in this regard differ from Amato and Luisi (2006), who find a strong positive relationship between spreads and financial activity, with size increasing for longer maturities.

While real activity and financial activity have comparable, albeit stronger, absolute impacts on the BBB curve, shocks to inflation affect the BBB curve differently than the other two rating categories. Starting with a significant negative impact, responses to positive shocks to inflation converge to zero for mid-term maturities, and only change signs for the long end of the BBB spread curve. Normally, inflation would be expected to have a stronger positive impact on lower-rated bonds. Parts of this effect, however, are captured by Latent 2, which has a very strong positive impact on BBB spreads and an almost negligible one on AA and A spreads. This leads to the conclusion that other systematic forces are driving the BBB credit spread curve.

Finally, note that Latent 3 has a negative impact, with increasing absolute size on all spread curves. This implies that a negative shock to Latent 3 leads to a widening of credit spreads, which is stronger for longer maturities. One interpretation is that other macroeconomic variables not included in this model have a significant impact on the term structures of credit spreads. One candidate for such a variable is market liquidity, as it has a major impact on spreads, especially after the beginning of the financial crisis in mid-2007.

The second method to show impulse responses from shocks to the state factors is to analyze the effect of a one-time shock over a continuous time span. Figures 2-6 to 2-11 illustrate the impulse responses of yields and credit spreads with different maturities to one-time shocks to the six state factors during a sixty-month period after the initial shock. Next the impulse responses of credit spreads to the three observable factors are discussed, as this is the main focus of this study (see Figures 2-6 to 2-8).

Figure 2-6: Impulse responses to the financial factor

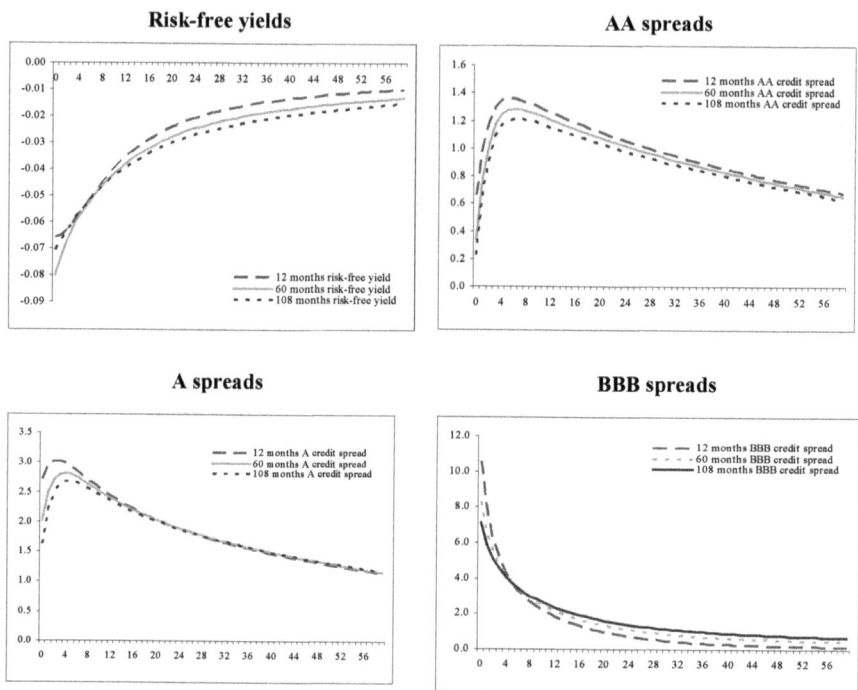

These figures show the responses of the respective yield and credit spread time series to a one-time, one-standard deviation shock to the financial factor. The x-axis shows the number of months since the one-time shock; the y-axis shows the responses in annualized percentages and basis points for the risk-free yields and credit spreads, respectively.

First, consider a positive shock to the financial factor, i.e., an increase in leverage, interest rate coverage, and volatility, and a decrease in cash flow. Shocks to this factor are quite persistent for AA and A spreads, but at a very low level. After a low immediate impact, credit spreads widen until four months after the shock, and stay at a higher level with a slow convergence to zero. This implies that the effect of shocks to financial activity on highly rated bonds is very limited in size, but has a significant long-term effect. In contrast, positive shocks to financial activity have a much stronger immediate impact on BBB spreads. However, the long-term impact converges to zero relatively quickly afterward.

Figure 2-7: Impulse responses to the real activity factor

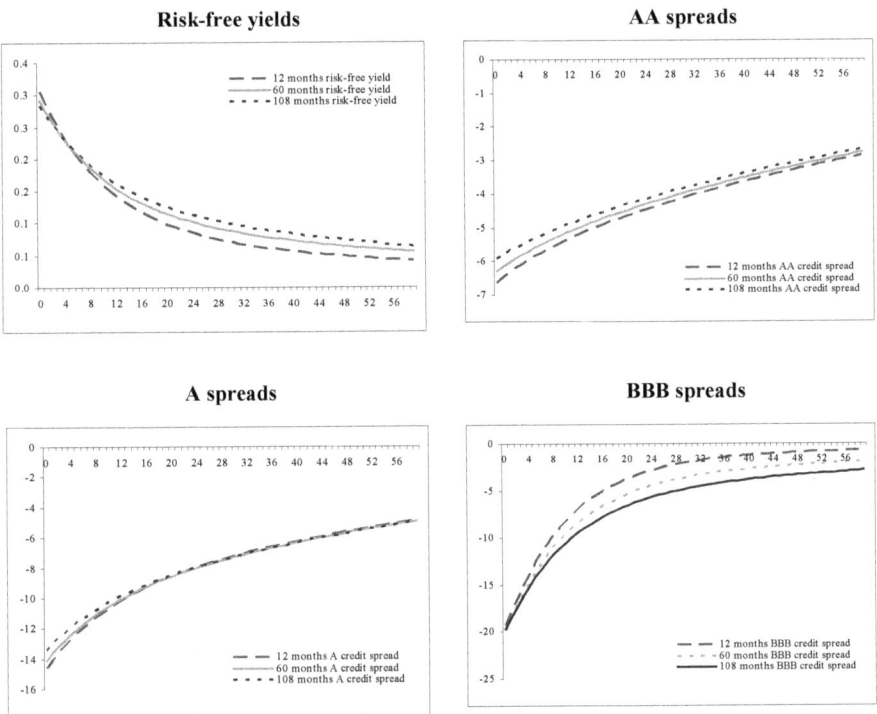

These figures show the responses of the respective yield and credit spread time series to a one-time, one-standard deviation shock to the real activity factor. The x-axis shows the number of months since the one-time shock; the y-axis shows the responses in annualized percentages and basis points for the risk-free yields and the credit spreads, respectively.

For real activity, the impulse responses are very similar for all rating categories. In line with the theory that positive impulses to the economy lead to decreasing credit spreads due to decreasing default risks, negative immediate responses for all rating classes are observed, with decreasing absolute sizes for better ratings. For all three rating categories, the immediate impact decreases in a strongly monotone function and converges to zero, with the BBB credit spread exhibiting the strongest relative convergence.

Figure 2-8: Impulse responses to the inflation factor

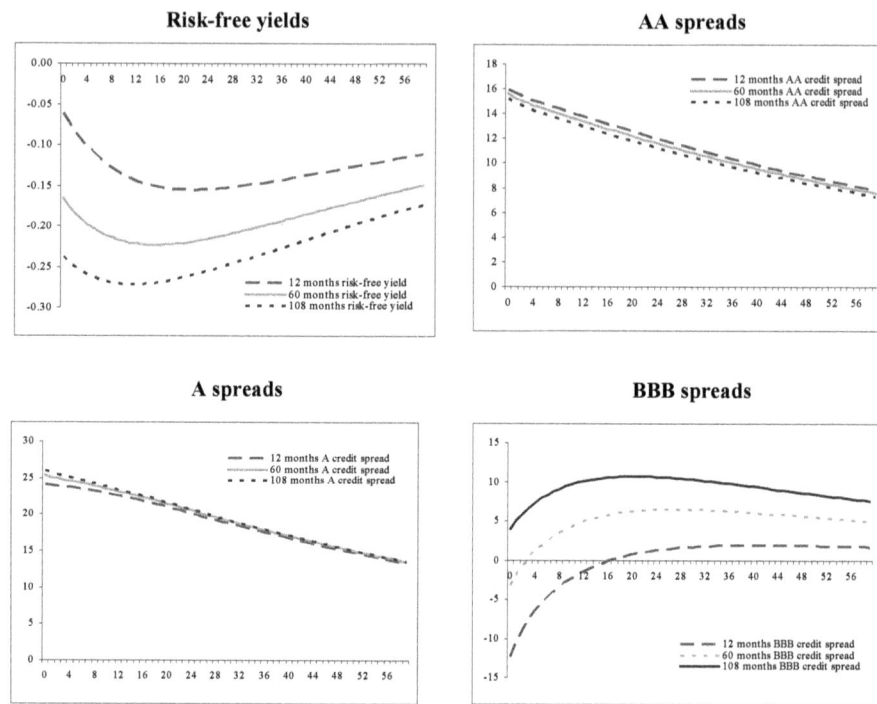

These figures show the responses of the respective yield and credit spread time series to a one-time, one-standard deviation shock to the inflation factor. The x-axis shows the number of months since the one-time shock; the y-axis shows the responses in annualized percentages and basis points for the risk-free yields and the credit spreads, respectively.

In line with the observation about the immediate responses described above, the inflation factor exhibits different behavior for AA and A spreads than for BBB spreads. For AA and A, the strong immediate impact decreases in an almost linear function over time, and stays at a high level even after sixty months. Thus, a positive shock to inflation leads to a widening of credit spreads not only as an immediate reaction, but also over a significant time horizon.

In contrast, the BBB curve shows different responses for short and long maturities. The initial negative responses for short-term and mid-term spreads change signs after some periods, which is not consistent with the theory that increased inflation results in the widening of spreads.[17] The overall effect, however, stays at a low level.

Figure 2-9: Impulse responses to the first latent factor

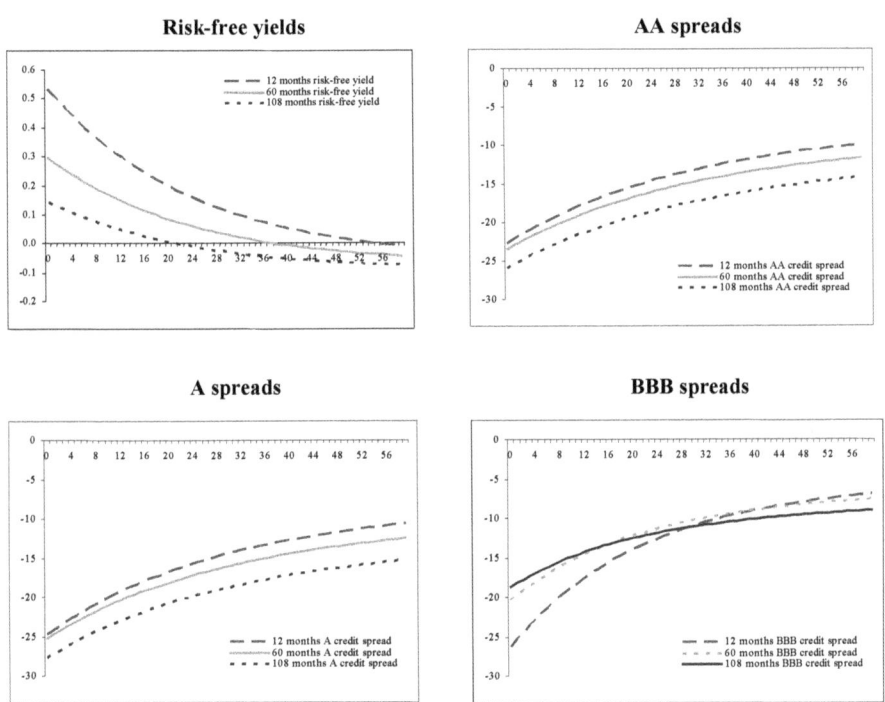

These figures show the responses of the respective yield and credit spread time series to a one-time, one-standard deviation shock to the first latent factor. The x-axis shows the number of months since the one-time shock; the y-axis shows the responses in annualized percentages and basis points for the risk-free yields and the credit spreads, respectively.

---

17   The time periods are three months after the initial shock for sixty-month BBB credit spreads, and sixteen months after the initial shock for twelve-month BBB credit spreads.

Figure 2-10: Impulse responses to the second latent factor

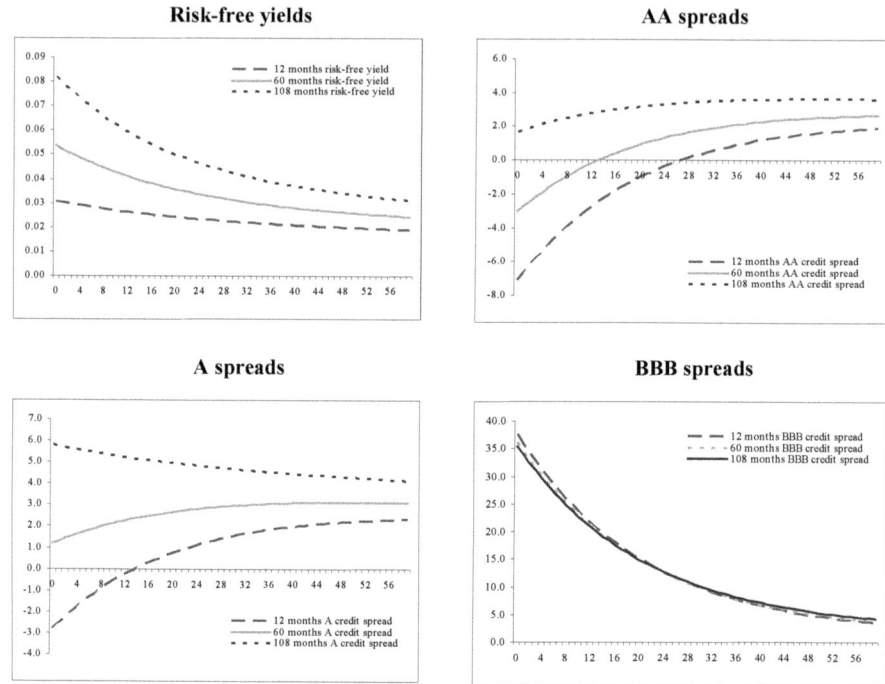

These figures show the responses of the respective yield and credit spread time series to a one-time, one-standard deviation shock to the second latent factor. The x-axis shows the number of months since the one-time shock; the y-axis shows the responses in annualized percentages and basis points for the risk-free yields and the credit spreads, respectively.

Finally, note that the impulse responses to Latents 1 and 3 are comparable for all spreads of the three rating classes. Only Latent 2 exhibits large differences between AA and A on the one hand, and BBB on the other. This again supports the hypothesis that Latent 2 captures parts of the inflation effect for BBB spreads.

Figure 2-11: Impulse responses to the third latent factor

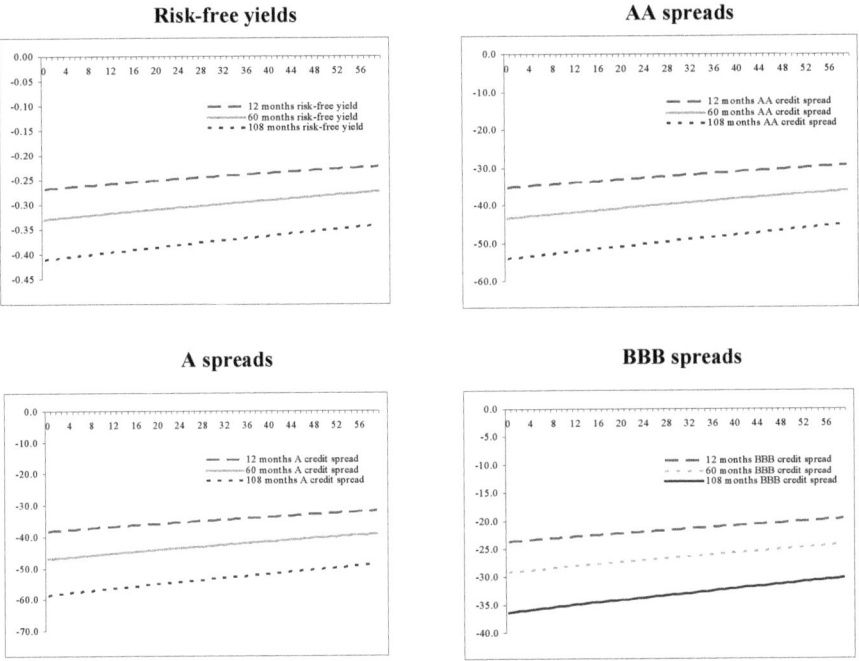

These figures show the responses of the respective yield and credit spread time series to a one-time, one-standard deviation shock to the third latent factor. The x-axis shows the number of months since the one-time shock; the y-axis shows the responses in annualized percentages and basis points for the risk-free yields and the credit spreads, respectively.

2.4.3 Variance Decompositions

To analyze the relative importance of the six state factors in the term structure model, the variance decomposition, i.e., the share of the forecast error variance that is attributable to each observable and latent factor, is computed next. Table 2-5 presents the results.

Consistent with the existing term structure literature that includes both observable and unobservable variables, both classes significantly contribute to the total forecast error variance of risk-free yields and credit spreads. First, for risk-free yields, real activity explains the largest part (about 15% to 35%) of the total variance among all macro variables, with decreasing values for increasing forecast horizons. Inflation has explanatory power only for thirty-six- and sixty-month yields, and the share increases with increasing forecast horizons.

In contrast to real activity and inflation, financial activity accounts for almost none of the variation in forecast errors of risk-free yields. The relative importance of real activity in explaining the conditional variance of risk-free yields is in line with the findings of Amato and Luisi (2006). In contrast to the estimates in this study, however, they find financial activity has much stronger explanatory power, and inflation has a significantly lower impact.

Table 2-5: Variance decompositions of yields and spreads

Maturity	Forecast horizon k	Latent Factor 1	Latent Factor 2	Latent Factor 3	Financial Activity	Real Activity	Inflation	Sum of Macro Factors
					Risk-free			
3	3	0.75	0.00	0.02	0.01	0.22	0.00	0.23
	12	0.76	0.00	0.03	0.02	0.18	0.00	0.21
	36	0.73	0.00	0.06	0.02	0.16	0.03	0.21
	60	0.69	0.00	0.09	0.02	0.15	0.04	0.22
12	3	0.72	0.00	0.03	0.04	0.21	0.01	0.26
	12	0.71	0.00	0.04	0.04	0.18	0.02	0.25
	36	0.65	0.00	0.07	0.04	0.17	0.07	0.27
	60	0.60	0.00	0.10	0.04	0.16	0.10	0.30
36	3	0.56	0.00	0.05	0.08	0.28	0.03	0.39
	12	0.55	0.00	0.07	0.07	0.25	0.07	0.38
	36	0.45	0.00	0.11	0.06	0.22	0.15	0.43
	60	0.39	0.01	0.15	0.05	0.21	0.19	0.46
60	3	0.40	0.01	0.08	0.10	0.35	0.07	0.52
	12	0.36	0.01	0.10	0.08	0.32	0.13	0.53
	36	0.26	0.01	0.16	0.07	0.27	0.24	0.57
	60	0.21	0.01	0.20	0.06	0.24	0.28	0.58
					AA spreads			
12	3	0.59	0.02	0.20	0.00	0.05	0.13	0.18
	12	0.57	0.02	0.23	0.01	0.05	0.14	0.19
	36	0.52	0.01	0.28	0.01	0.04	0.14	0.19
	60	0.49	0.01	0.32	0.01	0.04	0.14	0.18
36	3	0.58	0.01	0.24	0.00	0.04	0.12	0.17
	12	0.55	0.01	0.27	0.01	0.04	0.13	0.17
	36	0.51	0.00	0.32	0.01	0.04	0.13	0.17
	60	0.48	0.00	0.36	0.01	0.04	0.12	0.16
60	3	0.57	0.00	0.28	0.00	0.04	0.11	0.15
	12	0.54	0.00	0.30	0.01	0.04	0.11	0.15
	36	0.50	0.00	0.35	0.01	0.03	0.11	0.15
	60	0.47	0.00	0.39	0.01	0.03	0.10	0.14

Maturity	Forecast horizon k	Latent Factor 1	Latent Factor 2	Latent Factor 3	Financial Activity	Real Activity	Inflation	Sum of Macro Factors
				A spreads				
12	3	0.46	0.00	0.16	0.02	0.15	0.21	0.38
	12	0.44	0.00	0.18	0.03	0.13	0.23	0.38
	36	0.40	0.00	0.22	0.02	0.11	0.25	0.38
	60	0.38	0.00	0.25	0.02	0.10	0.25	0.36
36	3	0.45	0.00	0.19	0.02	0.14	0.21	0.36
	12	0.43	0.00	0.21	0.02	0.12	0.22	0.36
	36	0.39	0.00	0.25	0.02	0.10	0.24	0.36
	60	0.37	0.00	0.28	0.02	0.09	0.23	0.34
60	3	0.44	0.00	0.22	0.01	0.12	0.20	0.34
	12	0.42	0.00	0.24	0.02	0.11	0.21	0.34
	36	0.39	0.00	0.28	0.02	0.09	0.22	0.33
	60	0.37	0.00	0.31	0.02	0.08	0.21	0.31
				BBB spreads				
12	3	0.34	0.30	0.04	0.13	0.16	0.03	0.32
	12	0.40	0.32	0.06	0.07	0.13	0.02	0.22
	36	0.44	0.30	0.11	0.05	0.10	0.01	0.16
	60	0.44	0.27	0.15	0.04	0.09	0.01	0.14
36	3	0.29	0.33	0.06	0.12	0.19	0.01	0.32
	12	0.34	0.34	0.08	0.07	0.16	0.00	0.23
	36	0.37	0.31	0.14	0.05	0.12	0.01	0.18
	60	0.38	0.27	0.19	0.04	0.10	0.01	0.16
60	3	0.26	0.35	0.08	0.11	0.21	0.00	0.32
	12	0.29	0.35	0.11	0.07	0.17	0.00	0.25
	36	0.32	0.30	0.18	0.05	0.13	0.02	0.20
	60	0.33	0.26	0.23	0.04	0.11	0.03	0.18

This table shows the percentage of the k-period forecast error variance for different maturities of risk-free yields and credit spreads that is explained by the three latent and the three observed macro factors. The last column shows the forecast error variance that is explained by the three observed macro factors.

Latent 1 captures most of the variance explained by the latent factors, with a maximum share of 76% for the three-month yield and a forecast horizon of twelve months. Latent 2 explains almost none of the forecast error variance for all yields.

Overall, the share of forecast error variance explained by macro factors is comparably low for short maturities (approximately 20%). It rises, however, to a significant share of 50% to 60% for yields with a sixty-month time to maturity. Again in contrast, Amato and Luisi (2006) find that a much lower share of conditional variance for long-term yields is explained by macro factors. Their macro factors have more explanatory power for short maturities, but it declines sharply for long maturities.

For AA spreads, the explanatory power of the observable macro factors is generally quite low. Only 14% to 19% of total forecast error variances are explained, with inflation being the largest contributor. The share declines with increasing maturity. Most of the variance (more than 80%) is explained by Latents 1 and 3, while the relative importance of Latent 3 (Latent 1) increases (decreases) for increasing (decreasing) forecast horizons. The total variance of AA spreads explained by macro factors is comparable to that found by Amato and Luisi (2006) for BBB spreads (their best rating category). The distribution among macro factors differs, however, because financial activity contributes the most to conditional variance.

For A credit spreads, the total share explained by the macro factors is considerably higher, 31% to 38%. Again, inflation explains most (approximately one-fifth), while the rest is explained by real activity, and financial activity is almost irrelevant. Note that the 62% to 69% of total variance explained by latent factors is only driven by Latents 1 and 3. As with risk-free yields and A spreads, Latent 2 explains basically none of the variance.

In line with the results from impulse response functions, Latent 2 is closely linked to the BBB spreads, and replaces the contributions of the inflation factor and of Latent 3. Here, Latent 2 explains approximately one-third of the variations of the BBB spreads. Also, innovations to the financial factor can explain significantly more of the variation of BBB spreads than of the variation of the other yields and spreads. Financial activity explains up to 13% of forecast error variances.

In contrast, inflation has almost no explanatory power for BBB spreads. This result is in line with the discussions of the impulse response functions above. Real activity, however, is responsible for a substantial part of the variation, especially for long maturities. Overall, the explanatory power of macro variables for the variation of BBB credit spreads (14% to 36%) is between that of A and AA spreads.

In summary, financial activity explains a much larger share of forecast error variances in Amato and Luisi's (2006) model than in this model. But this study finds more explanatory power for real activity and inflation. This is linked to the low persistence of the financial activity factor in this model, which is expressed by the autocorrelation coefficient of 0.59, significantly below the 0.97 value (in discrete time) estimated by Amato and Luisi (2006).

This study also finds that a significant share of the conditional variances of credit spreads is explained by observable macro factors. For A spreads, this reaches a maximum of 38%. Across all rating categories, all maturities, and all forecast horizons, observable macro factors explain 24% of conditional forecast error variances of credit spreads in this model on average. This result is almost identical to Amato and Luisi's (2006) findings, who find that 25% of forecast error variances is explained by observable factors across all rating categories on average.

2.5 Conclusion

This study has built a macro-finance term structure model of credit spreads for the European bond market with observable and latent factors. Much of the methodology and variables used by Amato and Luisi (2006) were adopted, who in turn used the framework suggested by Ang and Piazzesi (2003). This is the first study to test an affine term structure model of credit spreads with observable macro variables for Europe. Additionally, it contributes to macro-finance literature, especially in regard to whether the European bond market is integrated.

The degree of integration of the European bond market is indirectly examined by comparing the results of this study to those of Amato and Luisi (2006). This is because they test a similar model for the U.S. market, considered the most integrated bond market worldwide. The parameters that are linked to the observable macro factors mostly have reasonable economic interpretations. The analyses of the impulse response functions and variance decompositions illustrate that yields and credit spreads react to variations in the underlying risk factors. The elements for the market price of risk are also significant, which shows that the term structure of credit spreads and yields can be at least partially explained by the model of this study.

It can be concluded that the macro-finance approach of modeling credit spreads for the European market yields results in line with similar models tested on the U.S. market. Consequently, it can be assumed that the basic principle of the law of one price seems largely to hold, and that financial integration is not far from the U.S. level.

There are, however, several deviations in the structure of the results in this study compared to the findings of Amato and Luisi (2006). Not all risk factors in this model are found to contribute uniformly to the market risk premiums. Additionally, the curvature of the credit spread curves cannot be accurately explained by latent factors. Both indications imply that the observable and latent factors cannot explain the complete shape of the term structure of credit spreads in the same way that they do in Amato and Luisi's (2006) U.S. model, despite the fact that similar methodology and data are used. One explanation for this is that European bond market financial integration is still below levels seen in the U.S., and that residual segmentation may lead to partial violations of the law of one price. This in turn results in credit spread deviations that cannot be explained by common risk factors.

Furthermore, the data set of this study includes the beginning of the financial crisis, and some clear indications of structural differences are found between the results of this study and those of comparable pre-crisis studies. Compared to Amato and Luisi's (2006) results, the parameters of the market price of risk indicate that credit spread deviations are characterized much more by parallel shifts of the entire spread curve in response to systematic shocks in underlying risk factors. The impulse response analyses of shocks to the state factors also support this.

Additionally, the third latent factor in this model seems to represent some systematic macroeconomic risk factor that impacts the credit spreads of all rating categories similarly. This is deduced from impulse responses to shocks to Latent 3, as well as from regression analyses of the level and slope of credit spread curves. It is concluded that other macroeconomic variables not represented by the macro factors have a significant impact on the term structure of credit spreads during the observation period. One explanation for this could be that market liquidity changes drive credit spreads, especially during the financial crisis that began during the second half of 2007.

Future research on macro-finance term structure models for the European bond market could logically explore two directions. First, the model setup could be extended to incorporate a more structural modeling of the macro module, including long-term expectations such as in Dewachter and Lyrio (2006), or interactions between risk factors and yields such as in Diebold *et al.* (2006), Hördahl *et al.* (2006), and Rudebusch and Wu (2008).

Second, the set of macroeconomic variables could be expanded to explain parts of the effects captured by latent factors in this model, and to better reflect the shape of the economy. It would be especially interesting to analyze how market liquidity changes impact credit spreads, and how this has changed since the start of the financial crisis.

3 Study 2: Has Liquidity Risk for Bonds Increased During the Financial Crisis? A Study for the European Corporate Bond Market

3.1 Introduction

During the recent global financial crisis, liquidity has become a major topic of interest for banks, investment vehicles, and regulators. Decreasing asset prices have led to huge write-offs within the financial sector with the result of a sharply falling capitalization within the sector and many situations where banks nearly or actually collapsed. Often, the required write-offs were not fully caused by defaults of the underlying debtors but by decreasing mark-to-market or mark-to-model valuations of the assets. One major reason for the falling asset prices was the illiquidity of single positions or whole asset classes like collateral debt obligations or, more generally, asset-backed securities.

Before the start of the financial crisis, the regulatory framework in Europe, summarized in the Basel II accord issued by the Basel Committee on Banking Supervision, did not deal appropriately with asset illiquidity and the resulting effects on asset prices. The major focus of Basel II was on credit risk, market risk and operational risk. While the impact of liquidity on asset valuations was at least theoretically considered as a sub-set of the market risk in the trading book, it almost did not matter in practice.

First, in the standardized approach of market risk for fixed income securities, the 2006 Basel II accord only addresses interest rate risk, foreign exchange risk and commodity risk. The capital charge for the specific risk of a security as part of the interest rate risk only depends on the credit rating, so that investment-grade bonds in fact have no capital charge for liquidity risk.[18]

Second, even if banks choose to calculate their market risk in the trading book according to the internal model approach, they mostly use conventional value-at-risk models that assume asset prices to depend on common risk factors such as interest rate risk, exchange rate risk, and rating migration. However, most of these models do not take into account the possibility of a sharp decline in liquidity for high quality assets.

---

18 The minimum capital requirements of the first pillar are detailed in Part 2 of the Basel II accord published by the Basel Committee on Banking Supervision (2006).

Overall, it is subsumed that the regulatory guidelines for capital requirements in the banking sector have not appropriately reflected liquidity risk as a part of the market risk of holding fixed income securities. Especially high-rated corporate bonds or bonds issued by financial institutions were regarded as more or less insensitive to liquidity risk with the result of very low capital requirements. In the aftermath of the financial crisis the ongoing discussion consequently centers on the discussion of how capital regulations should be altered to better reflect the liquidity risks of banks' trading books.

This study contributes to this discussion by examining the effect of liquidity on credit spreads and thus bond prices before and after the start of the financial crisis. It analyzes the impact of both bond-specific and market-wide liquidity on credit spread changes. Furthermore, it controls for various other bond-specific, firm-related, and market-related variables that may determine credit spread variations in the sample.

Based on structural break panel regression analyses of European corporate bonds, it is shown that liquidity has become much more relevant for credit spread variations and hence bond prices after the start of the financial crisis. Moreover, the study concludes that liquidity has become a more important source of risk for high-rated bonds and bonds issued by financial institutions.

The remainder of this paper is organized as follows. The next section reviews the existing literature on bond pricing and determinants of credit spreads and derives the theoretical background for the empirical research. Section 3.3 describes the corporate bond sample and the data used to construct the credit spreads. Furthermore the proxies for liquidity and the other control variables that enter the econometric estimations are described. Section 3.4 provides an overview of the empirical methods and discusses the estimation results. Section 3.5 gives the conclusions.

3.2 Theoretical Background and Related Literature

This section discusses the theoretical link between bond prices and credit spreads and the underlying factors that determine their variation.

3.2.1 Pricing of Defaultable Bonds

This study analyzes determinants of credit spreads. However, the following theoretical considerations deal with bond prices, which are also of interest for banks and regulators who want to evaluate asset portfolios. It is straightforward to link credit spreads and corporate bond prices and to show that both are essentially two sides of the same concept.

This can easily be shown if the pricing formula of a coupon paying defaultable bond is regarded. According to Longstaff et al. (2005), for example, the price of a corporate bond with maturity T, a continuous coupon rate c, and a recovery rate of 1-ω can be expressed as

$$B(c,\omega,T) = E\left[c\int_0^T \exp\left(-\int_0^t r_s + \lambda_s + \gamma_s \, ds\right) dt\right]$$
$$+ E\left[\exp\left(-\int_0^T r_t + \lambda_t + \gamma_t \, dt\right)\right] \qquad (3.1)$$
$$+ E\left[(1-\omega)\int_0^T \lambda_t \exp\left(-\int_0^t r_s + \lambda_s + \gamma_s \, ds\right) dt\right]$$

where r_t denotes the risk-free rate, λ_t the default intensity, and γ_t a convenience yield investors require beyond compensation for the credit risk captured by λ_t. Note, that γ_t may include the liquidity premium analyzed in this study. For the purpose of this study, the credit spread of a defaultable bond is defined as the difference between the yields to maturity of the corporate bond and a risk-free government bond with matching times to maturity. Hence, it can be concluded from Equation (3.1) that the credit spread, which is expressed as $\lambda_t + \gamma_t$, is positively related to the bond yield and negatively related to the bond price. This means that a widening credit spread is equal to a depreciation of the bond price and vice versa.

According to Takahashi et al. (2001) or Van Landschoot (2008), bond pricing models can be separated into two categories: structural models and reduced-form models.

Structural models build on the seminal contributions of Black and Scholes (1973) and Merton (1974) and were further developed by Black and Cox (1976), Leland (1994), Longstaff and Schwartz (1995), and Collin-Dufresne and Goldstein (2001), among many others. The underlying principle of structural models is that a corporate bond has the same payoff structure as the combination of a risk-free bond and short position in a put on the firm's assets with a strike price that is equal to the face value of the outstanding debt. Accordingly, determinants of bond prices in all variations of structural models are exclusively linked to the default risk of the bond issuer.[19] Hence, these models include the same factors

---

19 See, e.g., Cossin and Pirotte (2001) for an overview of various extensions of structural models.

that drive the values of risk-free bonds and equity options, namely the leverage ratio, volatility, and the risk-free interest rate.

To overcome the shortcomings of structural models, Jarrow and Turnbull (1995), Duffie and Singleton (1999), or Hull and White (2000), among others, introduced the class of reduced-form models. They try to model the default event exogenously based on a default intensity process, which is a function of (latent) state variables. Arora *et al.* (2005) argue that reduced-form models are often preferred because they are mathematically tractable and do not require complete information about the default point and the expected recovery rate. While reduced-form bond pricing models are better suited to fitting credit spreads observed in the market by calibrating the model parameters (Collin-Dufresne *et al.* (2001) and Takahashi *et al.* (2001)), structural models offer, according to Collin-Dufresne *et al.* (2001), more insight into the fundamental drivers of credit spreads.

One major drawback of many structural models and also some reduced-form models is that they systematically underestimate observed credit spreads. This observation is often called the credit spread puzzle[20], and a growing quantity of literature tries to explain which risk factors other than default risk drive credit spreads. Elton *et al.* (2001) and Campello *et al.* (2008) show that yield spreads on corporate bonds are linked to risk factors, which are normally used for pricing equities, e.g. stock market factors, book-to-market ratios, or momentum factors. Additionally, Elton *et al.* (2001) or Longstaff *et al.* (2005) argue that different local taxes influence credit spreads, and Duffee (1998) or Collin-Dufresne *et al.* (2001) propose that the whole term structure of the yield curve, i.e. slope and convexity, may be relevant to explain credit spreads. Collin-Dufresne *et al.* (2001) and Zhang *et al.* (2009) also incorporate proxies for the change of the business climate and account for jump risk premiums. Several of these factors are included as control variables in the empirical analyses below.

3.2.2 Liquidity as Driver for Bond Prices and Credit Spreads

In addition to the risk factors discussed above, liquidity has been found to have a major impact on asset prices. Based on the early contributions of Amihud and Mendelson (1986) and subsequently Boudoukh and Whitelaw (1993) or Vayanos (1998), the notion emerged that investors demand a yield premium for illiquid assets as compensation for transaction costs.

---

20 See, e.g., Elton *et al.* (2001), Amato and Remolona (2003), Hull *et al.* (2005), Covitz and Downing (2007), or Chen *et al.* (2009), among others.

Several studies have found empirical evidence for the impact of liquidity on prices in the equity market (e.g., Amihud and Mendelson (1986), Brennan and Subrahmanyam (1996), Haugen and Baker (1996), Chordia *et al.* (2001), or Acharya and Pedersen (2005)).

For government bonds, a broad range of contributions found statistically significant liquidity premiums, which are measured based on different liquidity proxies. Amihud and Mendelson (1991) and Kamara (1994) use pairs of zero coupon bonds with matching times to maturity to eliminate the interest rate risk and Elton and Green (1998) find yield differences between U.S. Treasury bonds with high and low trading volume. Goldreich *et al.* (2005) and Krishnamurthy (2002) examine the difference between most recently issued and older U.S. Treasury bonds and find yield differences, which they attribute to liquidity differences.

The more relevant field of research for this study concerns the corporate bond market. There are several studies that analyze the impact of liquidity on bond yields and spreads for the U.S. corporate bond market. Collin-Dufresne *et al.* (2001) apply a heterogeneous parameter model and conclude that corporate bond spreads are partially driven by local supply and demand shocks. They find a statistically significant impact of their liquidity proxies on credit spreads. Longstaff *et al.* (2005) find that bond-specific liquidity and general bond market liquidity are strongly related to the time varying nondefault component of corporate credit spreads. Ericsson and Renault (2006) develop a structural bond valuation model that includes credit and liquidity risk and they show that liquidity spreads are positively correlated with default components of the yield spread. Covitz and Downing (2007) explore yield spreads on very short-term commercial papers and report that liquidity explains some of the variation in spreads. Chen *et al.* (2007) find that corporate credit spreads are significantly correlated with different liquidity proxies. Controlling for various theoretical determinants of credit spreads, they find that bond-specific illiquidity is positively related to yield spreads. Mahanti *et al.* (2008) construct a new liquidity measure based on trading activity of investors holding that bond and find that this measure has explanatory power for both transaction costs and price impact in the corporate bond market. Edwards *et al.* (2007) show that secondary transaction costs in the corporate bond market, which they estimate based on trade sizes, are related to liquidity measured by various bond characteristics.

For the European corporate bond market, there are less empirical studies of liquidity effects on credit spreads. Boss and Scheicher (2002) examine the determinants of credit spread changes of European corporate bonds, which they extract from the *Euro Credit Index* provided by JP Morgan. They find that changes in market-wide liquidity impact credit spreads of bonds of financial institutions but not of industrial companies. Diaz and Navarro (2002) study the relationship between yield spreads and the time to maturity in the Spanish corporate bond market and find that bond liquidity is related to the observed credit spreads. Analyzing the impact of several different liquidity proxies on excess corporate bond yields Houweling *et al.* (2005) find that liquidity is priced in euro-denominated corporate bonds. They build their bond sample on the *Euro-Aggregate Corporate Bond Index* published by Lehman Brothers. De Jong and Driessen (2006) show that expected corporate bond returns include premiums for liquidity risk because they respond to fluctuations in bond and equity market liquidity. They also use Lehman Brothers' euro indices to construct their corporate bond sample. Van Landschoot (2008) compares the determinants of corporate bond yield spreads between the U.S. and Europe. They construct their European bond sample from the *Merrill Lynch Euro Corporate Broad Market Index*. They find that changes in liquidity risk contribute significantly to yield spread changes and that liquidity is higher for U.S. corporate bonds than for euro-denominated corporate bonds. Using bond data from the *iBoxx Euro Bond Index* Castagnetti and Rossi (2008) analyze the determinants of credit spread changes based on a panel regression model with a multifactor error structure. They include market-wide liquidity as independent variable and find no significant impact of observable liquidity proxies on credit spread changes. Instead, they assume that an unobserved common factor is related to liquidity conditions in the bond market.

Building on these studies this study aims at analyzing the impact of liquidity on credit spreads for European corporate bonds. In this regard it contributes to the empirical research on the pricing of defaultable bonds. Furthermore, this study is related to the credit spread puzzle, especially regarding the existence of a liquidity premium that can explain the difference between observed bond yields and default risk adjusted theoretical yields.

Generally, two different aspects of liquidity can be distinguished. First, bond-specific liquidity drives bond prices and hence bond yields and credit spreads. Decreasing liquidity of a specific bond lets investors demand a higher expected yield due to the increased risk of holding that bond compared to holding a more liquid bond. The theoretical result from decreasing bond-specific liquidity is a lower bond price, a higher bond yield, and thus a widening of the bond's credit spread.

Second, overall market liquidity is included to capture the effects of market-wide changes of corporate bond liquidity on credit spreads. According to Longstaff *et al.* (2005), market-wide illiquidity of bonds can arise, for example, during periods of flights to quality with the effect that corporate bonds trade at a discount with regard to highly liquid Treasury bonds.[21] Thus, under the assumption that individual bond liquidity results from demand and supply of a specific bond, market-wide corporate bond liquidity expresses the general market preference for risky corporate bonds vis-à-vis riskless government bonds.

The reasoning to include both individual corporate bond liquidity and market-wide liquidity is supported by Longstaff *et al.* (2005) who find that both measures are important dimensions for credit spreads.

As discussed above, several other studies have found that liquidity indeed has a major impact on credit spreads. However, most of them account for the impact of liquidity with constant coefficient estimates in cross-sectional or time-series regression analyses as, e.g., in Collin-Dufresne *et al.* (2001), or Chen *et al.* (2007). Other studies propose to model and estimate liquidity as a process, as do e.g., Longstaff *et al.* (2005), or Ericsson and Renault (2006).

The novelty of the approach of this study is to examine how the recent financial crisis has changed the sensitivity of credit spreads in Europe with regard to liquidity. The study uses a structural break approach to test how large the ongoing effect of the financial crisis is on the impact of liquidity on credit spreads. In addition to this, the results are differentiated with regard to the bond issuers' sector (financial sector vs. non-financial sector) and the bond rating. In this regard this study contributes to the recently emerging literature on the effects of the global financial crisis.

With this approach, the financial crisis should be identified as a regime shift for the pricing of corporate bonds. The results should foster the discussion that regulators and banks have to rethink their risk management methods especially with regard to capital requirements. This is particularly relevant for assets that were before seen as almost riskless, such as high-rated bonds or bonds issued by financial companies.

3.3 Data

3.3.1 Corporate Bond Sample

For the empirical estimation a database of corporate bonds with bond- and issuer-specific data is constructed. The sample period is July 2001 through June 2009. At any monthly observation point those corporate bonds are used that are listed in the *iBoxx Corporate Index* of euro-denominated bonds. Because the

---

21 Since this study examines the effect of the financial crisis on credit spreads, market-wide liquidity is assumed to play a dominant role for bond pricing.

analysis should be conducted on a pure European bond sample, any bonds issued by non-EU companies are excluded. Furthermore, bonds are excluded if they have less than six consecutive monthly observations of credit spreads or the other bond- and issuer-specific variables described below.

The resulting sample represents an unbalanced, dated panel with monthly observations, because the cross-section of bonds differs during the time horizon of the analysis due to the varying index composition at the individual observation points. Overall, the panel contains 26968 observations with 96 observation points on the time dimension and 53 to 573 individual bonds on the cross-section dimension. See Table 3-1 for the summary statistics on the corporate bond sample.

Table 3-1: Summary statistics of corporate bond samples

	Mean	Std. dev.	Min	Max
Credit spread (bp)	125.7	144.9	-25.5	2874.1
Credit spread change (bp)	3.2	46.4	-1154.4	2134.2
Bid-ask spread (bp)	72.3	96.0	3.3	3142.4
Bid-ask spread change (bp)	2.4	34.5	-1808.6	1920.8
Coupon (%)	5.1	1.1	0.0	9.4
Years to maturity	7.2	5.0	1.0	49.8
Notional amount (EUR mn)	909.9	506.4	500.0	4400.0

This table reports the summary statistics of the corporate bond sample. The sample consists of bonds listed in the iBoxx Corporate Index of euro-denominated bonds during the period from July 2001 through June 2009. Overall, the unbalanced panel contains 26968 observations with 96 observation points on the time dimension and 53 to 573 individual bonds on the cross-section dimension.

The data are obtained from four different sources: index constituents' data from iBoxx, market data from Bloomberg and Thomson Reuters Datastream, and macroeconomic data from the statistical database of the ECB.

Besides the time-varying variables described below, which enter the regressions of credit spread changes as regressors, additional bond characteristics allow the further detailing in the credit spread analyses. Based on the iBoxx rating the bonds are categorized into the four credit classes AAA, AA, A, and BBB. Furthermore, the bond issuers are differentiated between financial institutions and non-financial corporates. To do so, the Sector Level 2 defined by iBoxx is used.

The next section explains how the credit spreads, the liquidity data, and the other control variables that enter the econometric estimation are constructed.

3.3.2 Credit Spreads

Credit spreads of the individual bonds in the sample are calculated as differences between the yield to maturity of the bonds and the respective government benchmark yield. The former corresponds to the iBoxx mid price, while the latter belongs to a government benchmark bond with an equivalent time to maturity or is estimated by linear interpolation if a bond with the exact time to maturity is not available. Both yields are obtained from Thomson Reuters Datastream.

Table 3-2: Panel unit root tests of credit spreads

	Level data		First differences	
Method	Statistic	Prob*	Statistic	Prob*
Null: Unit root (assumes common unit root process)				
Levin, Lin and Chu t	16.79	1.0000	-61.00	0.0000
Breitung t-stat.	34.40	1.0000	-2.04	0.0207
Null: Unit root (assumes individual unit root process)				
Im, Pesaran and Shin W-stat	11.47	1.0000	-41.58	0.0000
ADF - Fisher Chi-squared	1156.21	0.9827	7800.85	0.0000
PP - Fisher Chi-squared	952.09	1.0000	10146.01	0.0000

* Probabilities for Fisher tests are computed using an asymptotic Chi-squared distribution. All other tests assume asymptotic normality.

This table shows a summary of different panel unit root tests for levels and first differences of credit spreads. Individual effects and individual linear trends are used as exogenous variables. The maximum number of lags included in the test equations is automatically selected based on the SIC. Bandwidth parameters are computed using the Newey-West method and the Barlett kernel.

In order to test for stationarity in the credit spread time series various panel unit root tests are conducted. The tests account for individual effects and individual linear trends and select the number of lags for each cross section based on the Schwarz information criterion (SIC). Table 3-2 shows panel unit root tests for levels and first differences of credit spreads. The results indicate that the null of non-stationarity of credit spreads cannot be rejected. However, first differences of credit spreads are stationary at a 1% confidence level.[22] Hence, credit spread changes are used as dependent variable in the econometric analyses described below.

3.3.3 Liqidity Measures

The focus of this paper is to analyze the impact of liquidity on credit spreads against the background of the global financial crisis. As described above, two different measures of liquidity are regarded: the liquidity of the individual corporate bonds and the overall market liquidity.

There is a broad discussion about how to measure liquidity of corporate bonds. Most of the existing measures are based either on transaction data or on general bond characteristics.

The most important liquidity measure in the first category is the bid-ask spread, which is also used by Chen *et al.* (2007), Longstaff *et al.* (2005), Van Landschoot (2008), or Chordia *et al.* (2005), among others. Other transaction-related liquidity measures include trading volume, trade count, number of quotes, or different ratios between those measures (see e.g., Collin-Dufresne *et al.* (2001) or Chordia *et al.* (2001)). Fleming (2003) compares different liquidity measures and shows that for liquid assets such as Treasury bonds the bid-ask spread is the best measure to track liquidity changes. According to Mahanti *et al.* (2008), transaction data are, however, only suited as proxies for liquidity if markets are reasonably liquid and have continuous trading activity. Therefore, they suggest using latent liquidity for less liquid markets such as the corporate bond market. They define latent liquidity of a corporate bond as turnover of investors who hold that bond.

A different approach to overcome the issue of limited trading activity in the less liquid corporate bond market is to use bond characteristics as liquidity proxy. Longstaff *et al.* (2005), for example, propose to use the notional amount, the age of the bond, the time to maturity, or a dummy variable reflecting whether the bond is issued by a financial services company.

Despite the mentioned drawbacks of using transaction-related data, this empirical study uses relative bid-ask spreads for several reasons. First, using bond characteristics as a liquidity proxy is not feasible, because credit spread changes are examined. Therefore, differenced data have to be used for the explanatory variables, too. Second, the requirement of a reasonable level of trading activity is given by the setup of the bond sample. Only bonds with a notional amount of at

---

22 Only the Breitung unit root test rejects the null at the 2.5% confidence level.

least 500 million euro and a remaining time to maturity of at least one year are included in the iBoxx indices. Moreover, the index calculation is based on bid and ask quotes by eleven major investment banks[23], which are required to buy and sell every bond belonging to the index. The quotes are then validated with several filters and consolidated according to rigorous rules to ensure a reasonable accuracy of the published bond prices. Finally, the compelling method of using latent liquidity as a measure is not feasible due to the unavailability of the required data.

This study uses changes in the monthly averages of daily relative bid-ask spreads (ΔBAS_t), which are calculated as differences between the bid prices and the ask prices as percent of the midpoints. An increase of the average relative bid-ask spread of a bond is assumed to reflect lower liquidity for the corporate bond, which in turn lets investors demand a higher yield due to the increased risk of holding that bond. Hence, a positive parameter estimate for this variable is expected.

As opposed to idiosyncratic liquidity of individual corporate bonds market-wide liquidity reflects the general tradability across all corporate bonds. Existing literature describes different ways to measure market-wide liquidity. Ericsson and Renault (2006), Collin-Dufresne *et al.* (2001), and Longstaff *et al.* (2005), for example, use the yield difference between on-the-run and off-the-run Treasury bonds. However, this measure is based only on the government bond market without including the corporate bond market. Longstaff *et al.* (2005) use flows into money market funds and the total amount of corporate debt issued as proxies for market-wide liquidity in the corporate bond market. Both proxies, however, are rather indirect measures of liquidity and can be influenced by other market disturbances that are not necessarily related to liquidity changes.

Therefore, changes in the difference between the ten-year euro swap rate and the ten-year government bond yield ($\Delta SWAP_t$) are used as proxy for changes of market-wide liquidity, as suggested by Collin-Dufresne *et al.* (2001) and Castagnetti and Rossi (2008), among others. Collin-Dufresne *et al.* (2001) argue that swap market liquidity and corporate bond market liquidity are strongly interlinked. According to Castagnetti and Rossi (2008) this is because issuers of corporate bonds typically fund on the swap market. Hence, rising swap spreads are expected to indicate a decreasing liquidity in the corporate bond market due to investors' preference for less risky government bonds with the result of increasing credit spreads.

---

[23] These are ABN AMRO, Barclays Capital, BNP Paribas, Deutsche Bank, Dresdner Kleinwort, Goldman Sachs, HSBC, JP Morgan, Morgan Stanley, Royal Bank of Scotland and UBS Investment Bank.

3.3.4 Additional Control Variables

Based on the theoretical and empirical findings regarding determinants of corporate bond prices described above, the empirical analysis controls for a set of bond-specific, firm-specific and market-wide effects that could effect changes in credit spreads of corporate bonds.

Changes of bond-specific volatility ($\Delta Vola_t$): Bond-specific volatility is computed as historical twelve-month volatility of monthly returns of the corporate bonds. Investors should demand higher premiums for increasing riskiness of returns. Hence, the estimated parameter is expected to have a positive sign.

Rating migration ($\Delta Rating_t$): As in Castagnetti and Rossi (2008), a variable is included that takes a value of 1 for each downgraded rating category, a value of -1 for each upgraded rating category, and a value of 0 for an unchanged rating category. A downgrading (upgrading) of a corporate bond by the major rating agencies signals a higher (lower) probability of default and hence higher (lower) credit risk for investors, and consequently a widening (narrowing) of the credit spread. Thus, the parameter estimate should take a positive value.

Changes of leverage (ΔLev_t): In standard structural models of bond prices such as the Merton (1974) model, a company's leverage determines its default risk and hence the price of its debt. The leverage ratio of the bond issuers is calculated as total debt divided by common equity as reported by Bloomberg. An increase in leverage should reflect a higher probability of default for the bonds outstanding and therefore a positive parameter estimate is expected for that variable.

Changes of the risk-free rate (Δr_t): The discussion about the impact of the risk-free interest rate on credit spreads is twofold. Longstaff and Schwartz (1995) propose that a higher spot rate reduces the default probability of a firm through an increased risk-neutral drift of the firm value process and hence leads to decreasing spreads. Several empirical studies for the U.S. corporate bond market support this argument (e.g., Collin-Dufresne *et al.* (2001) or Chen *et al.* (2007), among others). Zhang *et al.* (2009), however, argue that a higher spot rate may also reflect a tightened monetary policy with the result of increasing default probabilities and widening credit spreads. De Bondt (2002) or Rottmann and Seitz (2008) confirm this for the European corporate bond market. The risk-free interest rate is approximated by Bloomberg data on the fair market yield curve of AAA EU government bonds. To match the average maturity of the bond sample the data of the fair market curve with a time to maturity of seven years is used.

Changes of the slope of the risk-free yield curve ($\Delta Slope_t$): According to Collin-Dufresne *et al.* (2001), an increase in the slope of the risk-free yield curve reflects the expectation of rising interest rates in the future and, in line with the argumentation above, should lead to decreasing credit spreads. Additionally, the authors argue that a steepening term structure may indicate an improved economic environment with the same effect on credit spreads. Zhang *et al.* (2009), however, argue that a steeper slope of the yield curve can also be a forecast of rising inflation and tightening monetary policy with the effect of increasing credit spreads. In line with Chen *et al.* (2007) and Collin-Dufresne *et al.* (2001), the slope of the yield curve is calculated as the difference between the ten-year and the two-year risk-free rate, which are derived from the fair market curves described above.

Changes of the curvature of the risk-free yield curve ($\Delta Convex_t$): As proposed by others (e.g., Collin-Dufresne *et al.* (2001) or Castagnetti and Rossi (2008)), the change of the convexity of the risk-free yield curve is included in addition to changes in its level and slope in order to account for a non-linear term structure. The convexity is approximated by the difference between the five-year and the average of the ten-year and the two-year risk-free rates.

Changes of equity market returns (ΔRet_t): Increasing stock market returns are theoretically linked to an improvement of the business climate and a deleveraging of companies, and thus decreasing default probabilities (see, e.g., Ericsson and Renault (2006) or Collin-Dufresne *et al.* (2001)). Therefore, changes of the monthly growth rate of the *EuroStoxx50* stock market index are included as a regressor and a negative relationship between this variable and changes in credit spreads is expected.

Changes of equity market volatility ($\Delta VSOXXI_t$): Structural models such as the Merton (1974) model propose that the price of a bond can be linked to a short position in a put option on the firm value. Increasing stock market volatility leads to increasing option values and hence decreasing bond values with the result of increasing credit spreads. According to Collin-Dufresne *et al.* (2001), this is also associated with increasing default probabilities. In line with Ericsson and Renault (2006), Collin-Dufresne *et al.* (2001) or Van Landschoot (2008), among others, an implied volatility index is used to represent stock market volatility. In this study this is the implied volatility index of the *EuroStoxx50*.

Changes of production ($\Delta Production_t$): In order to control for effects of business climate changes on credit spreads, the change of the annual growth rate of the *industrial production index* published by the ECB is included. According to Athanassakos and Carayannopoulos (2001), increasing industrial production signals rising economic activity and improved confidence of investors in the corporate sector. Hence, changes of production are expected to be negatively related to credit spreads changes.

Changes of producer prices (ΔPPI_t): In addition to industrial production Athanassakos and Carayannopoulos (2001) use inflation as a macroeconomic indicator. They propose that investors demand risk premiums for their investments in corporate bonds during periods of high inflation. Consequently, credit spread changes are assumed to be positively related to changes in inflation, which are measured as the annual growth rates of the *producer price index* published by the ECB.

Lagged market default premium (BBB_{t-1}): In line with Collin-Dufresne et al. (2001) and Castagnetti and Rossi (2008), a default premium variable that represents the state of the corporate bond market at the previous observation point is included. This lagged variable is calculated as the spread of the *iBoxx Corporate BBB Index* yield over the ten-year risk-free yield. A negative coefficient of the lagged market default premium would indicate a mean-reverting behavior of credit spreads.

3.4 Empirical Specification and Estimation Results

This section presents the different econometric analyses with regard to the impact of liquidity on credit spreads and discusses the estimation results. It starts with a basis regression that shows the effect of changes in bond-specific and market-wide liquidity on credit spread changes over the whole sample. In a second step a structural break analysis is conducted to test how the liquidity impact on credit spreads differs before and after the start of the financial crisis. Finally, it is analyzed how the influence of liquidity on credit spreads differs between credit qualities and sectors.

3.4.1 Basis Regression and Overall Impact of Liquidity

The empirical analyses start with a basis regression where the overall impact of liquidity changes on credit spread changes is examined. To control for other effects besides liquidity the additional bond-, firm-, and market-related variables described above are included. Given the unbalanced panel structure of the data with different aggregation levels the following equation is tested:

$$\Delta CS_{i,j,t} = c + \beta' X_{i,t}^B + \gamma' X_{j,t}^F + \delta' X_t^M + \varepsilon_{i,j,t}, \tag{3.2}$$

where $X_{i,t}^B$, $X_{j,t}^F$, and X_t^M include bond-specific, firm-specific, and market-wide variables, respectively. $\Delta CS_{i,j,t}$ represents the change of the credit spread of bond i, issued by firm j between months t-1 and t. The error terms $\varepsilon_{i,j,t}$ and the constant c are defined according to the chosen estimation approach described below.

Thus, the basis panel regression estimates the following equation:

$$\Delta CS_{i,j,t} = c + \beta_1 \Delta BAS_{i,t} + \beta_2 \Delta Vola_{i,t} + \beta_3 \Delta Rating_{i,t} + \gamma_1 \Delta Lev_{j,t} + \delta_1 \Delta Swap_t$$
$$+ \delta_2 \Delta r_t + \delta_3 \Delta Slope_t + \delta_4 \Delta Convex_t + \delta_5 \Delta Ret_t + \delta_6 \Delta VSTOXXI_t \quad (3.3)$$
$$+ \delta_7 \Delta Production_t + \delta_8 \Delta PPI_t + \delta_9 BBB_{t-1} + \varepsilon_{i,j,t}$$

In a panel setting with data of different corporate bonds, heteroscedasticity is a potential issue. Although the panel setup accounts for bond-specific data such as liquidity and volatility, different bonds in the sample can be traded in different market segments and thus the variance of residuals can vary between the individual bonds. Since heteroscedasticity violates the OLS assumptions with the result of non-robust standard errors, a White (1980) test is applied, where the squared OLS residuals are regressed on the cross product of the regressors and a constant. Both the White's test statistic as well as the LM statistic lead to a rejection of the null of homoscedastic residuals at 0% error probability. To account for heteroscedasticity in credit spread changes across different corporate bonds an estimated generalized least squares (EGLS) approach with cross-section weights is used.

In the EGLS estimation the error terms in Equations (3.2) and (3.3) allow for a different residual variance for each cross-section, while the covariance between residuals of different periods and different cross-sections is assumed to be 0:

$$E(\varepsilon_{i,t}\varepsilon_{i,t} | X_i) = \sigma_i^2$$
$$E(\varepsilon_{i,s}\varepsilon_{j,t} | X_i) = 0 \quad (3.4)$$

with $i \neq j$ and $s \neq t$.

Furthermore, period robust standard errors according to White (1980) are calculated to accommodate arbitrary serial correlation and time-varying variances.

Another problem with OLS or GLS estimations can arise if there are unobserved firm-specific effects in the panel data (see, e.g., Wooldridge (2007)), which have impact on credit spread changes and are not reflected in the leverage variable. Examples for those effects are the quality of management, sector-related differences between firms, or a firm-specific risk appetite. If these unobserved effects are correlated with the regressors of the model the residuals are correlated across bonds of the same firms and the model parameters cannot be consistently estimated. According to Wooldridge (2007), fixed effect specifications can be applied to account for these unobserved effects. Thereby, cross-section-specific means are removed from the exogenous regressors and from the dependent variable (Baltagi (2008)). In order to test for fixed effects at the firm level a redundant fixed effects test is applied by testing the joint significance of fixed effects in the basis OLS regression against the null hypothesis of an unrestricted specification. Both the cross-section F-statistic and the cross-section Chi-squared and their associated p-values reject the null of redundant fixed effects at the firm level. Consequently, firm-specific fixed effects estimators are used. Technically, the constant c of Equation (3.2) is replaced by the firm-specific fixed effect estimator c_j, because the constant and the fixed effect estimators cannot be separated. For convenience the fixed effect estimators are jointly reported for all firms as an intercept representing the weighted average of the individual estimators.

The results for OLS and EGLS estimates with and without firm-level fixed effects are reported in Table 3-3. Due to the above described statistical tests for heteroscedasticity and unobserved fixed effects, only the results of the EGLS panel regression with fixed effects on the firm-level are described.

Table 3-3: Basis panel regressions

Model	I: OLS			II: EGLS		
	Estimate		Std. err.	Estimate		Std. err.
Constant	5.2760	***	0.4712	3.5882	***	0.1507
Bond-specific						
ΔBAS_t	0.3048	***	0.0876	0.3454	***	0.0209
$\Delta Vola_t$	0.0332	**	0.0151	0.0223	***	0.0036
$\Delta Rating_t$	2.2982		3.6662	0.5646		1.1433
Firm-specific						
ΔLev_t	0.0009		0.0015	0.0008		0.0008
Market-wide						
$\Delta Swap_t$	0.8522	***	0.0713	0.6503	***	0.0286
Δr_t	0.4048	***	0.1442	0.2321	***	0.0632
$\Delta Slope_t$	-0.0795		0.1027	0.0239		0.0452
$\Delta Convex_t$	-0.5478	***	0.1403	-0.2967	***	0.0609
ΔRet_t	-0.0085	***	0.0010	-0.0037	***	0.0003
$\Delta VSTOXXI_t$	0.0115	***	0.0010	0.0093	***	0.0005
$\Delta Production_t$	-0.0342	***	0.0020	-0.0213	***	0.0007
ΔPPI_t	-0.0167	***	0.0042	-0.0085	***	0.0014
BBB_{t-1}	-0.0313	***	0.0030	-0.0226	***	0.0010

Model	III: OLS, fixed effects			IV: EGLS, fixed effects		
	Estimate		Std. err.	Estimate		Std. err.
Constant	5.6663	***	0.5171	4.4448	***	0.1772
Bond-specific						
ΔBAS_t	0.3005	***	0.0864	0.3402	***	0.0209
$\Delta Vola_t$	0.0291	*	0.0150	0.0207	***	0.0035
$\Delta Rating_t$	1.8545		3.6759	0.4649		1.1531
Firm-specific						
ΔLev_t	0.0004		0.0014	0.0007		0.0007
Market-wide						
$\Delta Swap_t$	0.8496	***	0.0712	0.6490	***	0.0287
Δr_t	0.4439	***	0.1463	0.2295	***	0.0633
$\Delta Slope_t$	-0.1085		0.1035	0.0251		0.0452
$\Delta Convex_t$	-0.5835	***	0.1422	-0.2944	***	0.0610
ΔRet_t	-0.0085	***	0.0010	-0.0037	***	0.0003
$\Delta VSTOXXI_t$	0.0114	***	0.0010	0.0093	***	0.0005
$\Delta Production_t$	-0.0339	***	0.0019	-0.0213	***	0.0007
ΔPPI_t	-0.0193	***	0.0044	-0.0091	***	0.0014
BBB_{t-1}	-0.0330	***	0.0030	-0.0229	***	0.0010

This table reports the results of the basis regressions. Credit spread changes are regressed against changes of bond-specific and market-wide liquidity and a set of control variables. The unbalanced panel includes 95 monthly observations from August 2001 through June 2009, 630 cross-sections, and a total number of 26338 observations. Four different models are shown: OLS estimations with and without firm-level fixed effects and EGLS estimations with and without firm-level fixed effects. In addition to the parameter estimates White robust standard errors and associated significance levels are reported. *** (**, *) denotes significant parameters at a 1% (5%, 10%) significance level.

The preliminary findings of the basis regressions confirm the expectations and existing empirical studies regarding the effect of liquidity on credit spreads. During the entire time period and across all bonds, changes in both the bond-specific illiquidity, measured as the relative bid-ask spread (ΔBAS_t), and market-wide illiquidity, measured as the swap spread ($\Delta SWAP_t$), are positively and significantly related to credit spread changes. On average, if the bid-ask spread (swap spread) rises by 100 basis points, the credit spread increases by about 34 (65) basis points. Both parameter estimates are significant at a 1% confidence level. This finding is consistent with the hypothesis that investors demand a yield premium for less liquid corporate bonds and that a market-wide decline in corporate bond liquidity leads to a widening of credit spreads.

Also, most of the additional control variables are statistically significant and have the expected signs. Changes in bond return volatility ($\Delta Vola_t$) and changes in stock market volatility ($\Delta VSOXXI_t$) have, as expected, a significant and positive impact on credit spread changes, because the riskiness of bonds increases with positive shocks to both variables. Changes in stock market returns (ΔRet_t) and changes in production ($\Delta Production_t$) represent positive impulses to the business climate with the result of decreasing default probabilities and narrowing credit spreads.

The parameter estimate for changes of the risk-free rate (Δr_t) has a positive sign. Hence, the results support the arguments of Zhang et al. (2009) and De Bondt (2002) that credit spreads widen as a result of a rising spot rate because market participants expect increasing default probabilities due to a tightened monetary policy. The parameter estimate for the slope of the yield curve ($\Delta Slope_t$) is not significant in any of the basis regression models at conventional significance levels. The variable for changes of the term structure convexity ($\Delta Convex_t$), however, has a significantly negative impact on credit spread changes.

The coefficient for the market default premium (BBB_{t-1}) is negative and statistically significant. Thus, empirical evidence confirms the findings of Collin-Dufresne et al. (2001) and Castagnetti and Rossi (2008) and it is concluded that credit spreads exhibit a mean-reverting behavior.

Interestingly, neither the rating migration ($\Delta Rating_t$) nor leverage changes (ΔLev_t) seem to have a significant impact on credit spread changes, although both variables directly measure credit risk. The statistical insignificance of the leverage variable can partially be explained by the data. Because not all companies in the sample are publicly listed, balance-sheet data has been used to calculate the ratio of debt to equity where the theoretically correct market values were not available.

Finally, note that the coefficient for inflation changes (ΔPPI_t) has a significantly negative sign. This finding rejects the hypothesis that inflationary pressure leads to rising credit spreads because investors demand higher risk premiums.

3.4.2 Structural Break Analysis

Having confirmed that market-wide and bond-specific illiquidity generally leads to widening credit spreads, the effect of the start of the financial crisis on the relationship between liquidity and credit spreads is analyzed in the following.

While increasing subprime mortgage defaults in the U.S. in February 2007 are seen as the trigger for the subsequent financial crisis, the collapse of two hedge funds of Bear Stearns, the dry-up in the market of short-term asset backed securities, and the near failing of the German bank IKB are considered to be the starting point of the global crisis.[24] All three events happened in July 2007, so that this month is taken as the break point for the subsequent analyses. It should be mentioned that the results do not differ much if any other break point between February and October 2007 is chosen. Figure 3-1 also confirms the extreme widening of average European credit spreads as a result from the start of the financial crisis in 2007.

Figure 3-1: Time series of credit spreads for different rating categories

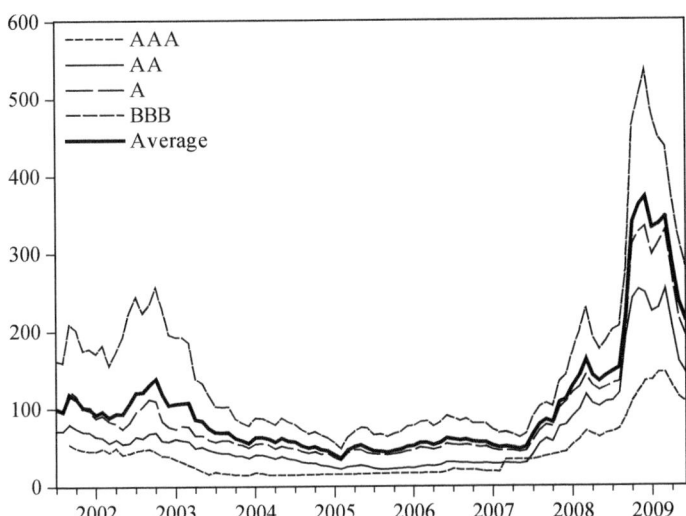

This figure shows the time series of average credit spreads of the corporate bond sample in basis points. Credit spreads are calculated as the differences between the yields to maturity of corporate bonds and government benchmark bonds with corresponding time to maturity.

A Chow (1960) breakpoint test[25] validates that July 2007 represents a structural break point for the basis regression presented above. Based on the test's F-statistic the null hypothesis that July 2007 is not a structural breakpoint cannot be rejected.

---

24 See, e.g., Brunnermeier (2009) for a summary of the progress of the global financial crisis.
25 The test compares the sum of squared residuals of a single estimation over the entire sample with the sum of squared residuals of separate estimations over the pre- and the post-breakpoint subsamples.

This result leads to the analysis of the effects of the financial crisis on the credit spread determinants with a time dummy variable. A dummy variable is included in the panel regression that takes a value of 0 for all observation points before July 2007 and a value of 1 for July 2007 and all subsequent months. With this, the ongoing effects of the financial crisis after its start are tested under the assumption that the implications of the crisis on credit spreads have not yet returned to pre-crisis levels towards the end of the observation period.

The specification accounts for shifts in the intercept and the slopes of the regression, so that the regression coefficients become time dependent. Therefore, the test equation can be expressed as

$$\Delta CS_{i,j,t} = c(t) + \beta'(t) X^B_{i,t} + \gamma'(t) X^F_{j,t} + \delta'(t) X^M_t + \varepsilon_{i,j,t}$$

$$\Theta(t) = \begin{cases} \Theta_1 & t < t_{break} \\ \Theta_1 + \Theta_2 & t \geq t_{break} \end{cases}, \quad (3.5)$$

$$\Theta \equiv c, \beta, \gamma, \delta$$

where $\Delta CS_{i,j,t}$, $X^B_{i,t}$, $X^F_{j,t}$, and X^M_t are defined as in Equation (3.2). Based on the preliminary results of the basis regression the model is estimated with an EGLS panel regression approach including fixed effects on the firm-level.

Inserting the explanatory variables, the following equation is obtained:

$$\begin{aligned}\Delta CS_{i,j,t} = {}& c_{0,1} + \beta_{1,1} \Delta BAS_{i,t} + \beta_{2,1} \Delta Vola_{i,t} + \beta_{3,1} \Delta Rating_{i,t} + \gamma_{1,1} \Delta Lev_{j,t} \\&+ \delta_{1,1} \Delta Swap_t + \delta_{2,1} \Delta r_t + \delta_{3,1} \Delta Slope_t + \delta_{4,1} \Delta Convex_t + \delta_{5,1} \Delta Ret_t \\&+ \delta_{6,1} \Delta VSTOXXI_t + \delta_{7,1} \Delta Production_t + \delta_{8,1} \Delta PPI_t + \delta_{9,1} BBB_{t-1} \\&+ c_{0,2} DT + \beta_{1,2} DT\Delta BAS_{i,t} + \beta_{2,2} DT\Delta Vola_{i,t} + \beta_{3,2} DT\Delta Rating_{i,t} \\&+ \gamma_{1,2} DT\Delta Lev_{j,t} + \delta_{1,2} DT\Delta Swap_t + \delta_{2,2} DT\Delta r_t + \delta_{3,2} DT\Delta Slope_t \\&+ \delta_{4,2} DT\Delta Convex_t + \delta_{5,2} DT\Delta Ret_t + \delta_{6,2} DT\Delta VSTOXXI_t \\&+ \delta_{7,2} DT\Delta Production_t + \delta_{8,2} DT\Delta PPI_t + \delta_{9,2} DT BBB_{t-1} + \varepsilon_{i,j,t} \end{aligned} \quad (3.6)$$

where DT represents the time dummy described above.

Table 3-4 summarizes the regression results. The first column shows the parameter estimates for the credit spread determinants without the dummy variable. These estimates represent the pre-break coefficients. The second column shows the parameter estimates for the product of the structural break dummy variable and the credit spread determinants. Thus, they can be interpreted as estimates of the additional impact of the explanatory variables on credit spread changes after the start of the financial crisis. According to Equation (3.5) the total impact of the credit spread determinants during the financial crisis can be computed by adding up the pre-break and the post-break parameter estimates.

Table 3-4: Panel regressions with structural break dummies

	Pre-crisis				Post-crisis		
	Estimate		Std. err.		Estimate		Std. err.
Constant	1.5945	***	0.2130	DT	14.0906	***	0.7093
Bond-specific							
ΔBAS_t	0.1400	***	0.0291	$DT*\Delta BAS_t$	0.1576	***	0.0306
$\Delta Vola_t$	0.0003		0.0021	$DT*\Delta Vola_t$	0.0257	***	0.0058
$\Delta Rating_t$	0.7048		0.9753	$DT*\Delta Rating_t$	1.9187		2.3471
Firm-specific							
ΔLev_t	0.0003		0.0003	$DT*\Delta Lev_t$	0.0034		0.0027
Market-wide							
$\Delta Swap_t$	0.2051	***	0.0251	$DT*\Delta Swap_t$	0.4146	***	0.0487
Δr_t	0.1313	***	0.0374	$DT*\Delta r_t$	0.8335	***	0.1401
$\Delta Slope_t$	-0.0771	**	0.0307	$DT*\Delta Slope_t$	-0.4541	***	0.0940
$\Delta Convex_t$	-0.1355	***	0.0370	$DT*\Delta Convex_t$	-0.8553	***	0.1296
ΔRet_t	-0.0004		0.0003	$DT*\Delta Ret_t$	-0.0059	***	0.0006
$\Delta VSTOXXI_t$	0.0030	***	0.0004	$DT*\Delta VSTOXXI_t$	0.0094	***	0.0007
$\Delta Production_t$	-0.0002		0.0006	$DT*\Delta Production_t$	-0.0271	***	0.0011
ΔPPI_t	0.0001		0.0014	$DT*\Delta PPI_t$	-0.0584	***	0.0043
BBB_{t-1}	-0.0156	***	0.0021	$DT*BBB_{t-1}$	-0.0439	***	0.0033

This table shows the results of the structural break regression. Credit spread changes are regressed against changes of bond-specific and market-wide liquidity and a set of control variables. The time dummy variable DT is included as moderator variable in the panel regression. DT takes a value of 0 for all monthly observations from August 2001 through June 2007 and a value of 1 for July 2007 through June 2009. The unbalanced panel includes 95 monthly observations (71 before and 24 after the break), 630 cross-sections (421 before and 617 after the break), and a total number of 26338 observations (14219 before and 12119 after the break). The model is estimated with an EGLS approach and accounts for firm-level fixed effects. In addition to the parameter estimates White robust standard errors and associated significance levels are reported. *** (**, *) denotes significant parameters at a 1% (5%, 10%) significance level.

The results show that except for the rating migration and the changes in leverage[26], all explanatory variables have a statistically and economically significant impact on credit spread changes after the start of the financial crisis. In contrast, changes in bond volatility, market returns, production, and producer prices had no significant impact on credit spread changes during the pre-crisis period. Furthermore, the intercept of the regression has increased significantly after the

---

26 Both variables did not contribute significantly to variations in credit spread changes in the basis regression either.

break. Together, these results indicate that the financial crisis represents a significant regime shift for credit spreads and thus for bond prices.

A comparison of the results in Table 3-4 with the results of the basis regressions in Table 3-3 shows that the signs of the significant parameters are the same in the structural break regression and in the basis regressions discussed above. From Table 3-4 it can also be noted that all significant parameters have the same signs but larger absolute values for the post-crisis period compared to the pre-crisis period. Hence, the explanatory variables have affected credit spreads in the same direction throughout the whole observation period, but the size of the impact has substantially changed during the financial crisis. Specifically, the effect of equally strong shocks to the determinants of credit spread changes has more than doubled after the start of the financial crisis.

Figure: 3-2: Changes of average credit spreads and average relative bid-ask spreads

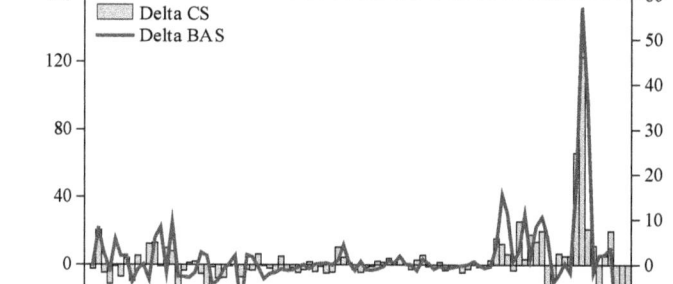

This figure shows the time series of average credit spread changes and average changes in relative bid-ask spreads of the corporate bond sample in basis points. Credit spreads are calculated as the differences between the yields to maturity of corporate bonds and government benchmark bonds with corresponding time to maturity. Relative bid-ask spreads are calculated as the monthly averages of daily differences between the bid prices and the ask prices as percent of the midpoints.

For bond-specific liquidity a 100 basis point increase of the bid-ask spread leads to a widening of credit spreads of 14 basis points before the financial crisis started. After the start the impact reinforces by 16 basis points, so that the total effect amounts to about 30 basis points. Thus, the impact of changes in bond-specific liquidity has relatively increased by 113% during the crisis. This effect is also illustrated in Figure 3-2, where changes in the relative bid-ask spread and changes in average credit spreads are depicted.

For market-wide liquidity the effect of the financial crisis is even stronger. While credit spreads have on average increased by 20 basis points in response to a 100 basis points increase in the swap spread, they widen by about 62 basis points during the crisis. This additional effect of 42 basis points represents a relative increase of about 200% for the impact of market-wide liquidity changes on credit spread changes. Figure 3-3 shows the correlation between changes in the swap spread and credit spread changes.

Figure 3-3: Changes of average credit spreads and average swap spreads

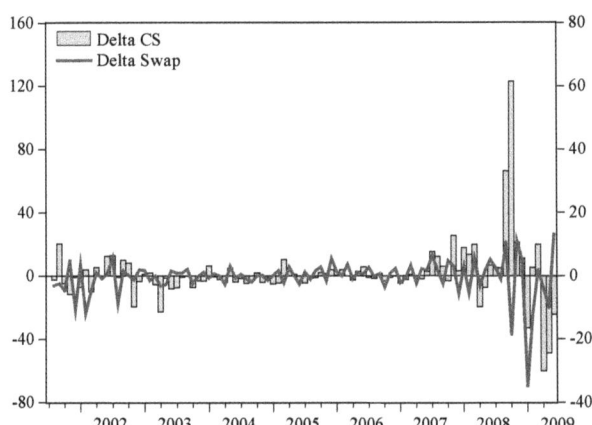

This figure shows the time series of average credit spread changes of the corporate bond sample and the changes in the swap spread in basis points. Credit spreads are calculated as the differences between the yields to maturity of corporate bonds and government benchmark bonds with corresponding time to maturity. The swap spread is calculated as the difference between the ten-year euro swap rate and the ten-year government bond yield.

As shown in Table 3-5 the described effects do not fundamentally change when the statistically insignificant variables in Equation (3.6) are dropped. Notably, the effects for bond-specific and market-wide liquidity described above are economically and statistically nearly the same.

Table 3-5: Parsimonious panel regressions with structural break dummies

Pre-crisis	Estimate		Std. err.		Post-crisis	Estimate		Std. err.
Constant	1.6554	***	0.2165	DT		13.8996	***	0.7072
Bond-specific								
ΔBAS_t	0.1387	***	0.0291	$DT*\Delta BAS_t$	0.1584	***	0.0308
$\Delta Vola_t$				$DT*\Delta Vola_t$	0.0259	***	0.0056
$\Delta Rating_t$				$DT*\Delta Rating_t$			
Firm-specific								
ΔLev_t				$DT*\Delta Lev_t$			
Market-wide								
$\Delta Swap_t$	0.2050	***	0.0248	$DT*\Delta Swap_t$	0.4126	***	0.0487
Δr_t	0.1261	***	0.0357	$DT*\Delta r_t$	0.8269	***	0.1384
$\Delta Slope_t$	-0.0708	**	0.0287	$DT*\Delta Slope_t$	-0.4535	***	0.0924
$\Delta Convex_t$	-0.1301	***	0.0350	$DT*\Delta Convex_t$	-0.8507	***	0.1279
ΔRet_t	0.0032	***	0.0004	$DT*\Delta Ret_t$	-0.0062	***	0.0005
$\Delta VSTOXXI_t$				$DT*\Delta VSTOXXI_t$	0.0093	***	0.0007
$\Delta Production_t$				$DT*\Delta Production_t$	-0.0273	***	0.0009
ΔPPI_t				$DT*\Delta PPI_t$	-0.0578	***	0.0042
BBB_{t-1}	-0.0161	***	0.0021	$DT*BBB_{t-1}$	-0.0429	***	0.0033

This table shows the results of the structural break regression with those variables having statistically significant coefficients at the 10% confidence level in the structural break regression. Credit spread changes are regressed against changes of bond-specific and market-wide liquidity and a set of control variables. The time dummy variable DT is included as moderator variable in the panel regression. DT takes a value of 0 for all monthly observations from August 2001 through June 2007 and a value of 1 for July 2007 through June 2009. The unbalanced panel includes 95 monthly observations (71 before and 24 after the break), 630 cross-sections (421 before and 617 after the break), and a total number of 26338 observations (14219 before and 12119 after the break). The model is estimated with an EGLS approach and accounts for firm-level fixed effects. In addition to the parameter estimates White robust standard errors and associated significance levels are reported. *** (**, *) denotes significant parameters at a 1% (5%, 10%) significance level.

3.4.3 Sector- and Rating-Specific Results

Table 3-6: Summary statistics of corporate bond subsamples

Subsample	I	II	A	B
Rating	AAA, AA	A, BBB	All	All
Sector	All	All	Financial	Non-Financial
No. of observations	5298	21040	9166	17172
ΔCS_t				
Mean	4.10	2.91	4.34	2.52
Std. dev.	39.58	47.95	54.82	41.17
Min	-347.63	-1154.42	-1154.42	-561.10
Max	2134.23	1318.60	2134.23	1120.12
ΔBAS_t				
Mean	2.61	2.40	3.26	2.01
Std. dev.	24.14	36.63	43.79	28.27
Min	-578.21	-1808.65	-797.09	-1808.65
Max	328.01	1920.76	1920.76	1065.74

Subsample	I.A	I.B	II.A	II.B
Rating	AAA, AA	AAA, AA	A, BBB	A, BBB
Sector	Financial	Non-Financial	Financial	Non-Financial
No. of observations	3858	1440	5308	15732
ΔCS_t				
Mean	5.14	1.31	3.75	2.63
Std. dev.	45.42	14.98	60.74	42.77
Min	-347.63	-78.95	-1154.42	-561.10
Max	2134.23	103.27	1318.60	1120.12
ΔBAS_t				
Mean	2.80	2.10	3.60	2.00
Std. dev.	26.92	14.24	52.77	29.22
Min	-578.21	-156.01	-797.09	-1808.65
Max	328.01	115.04	1920.76	1065.74

This table reports the summary statistics on the different subsamples used to differentiate the analysis with regard to the credit quality and the sector of the bond issuer. The iBoxx rating is used as a bond's rating class and the sector is assigned according to the Sector Level 2 in the iBoxx database. Changes in credit spreads and changes in relative bid-ask spreads are shown in basis points.

In order to analyze whether liquidity effects during the financial crisis are different with regard to the rating and/or the sector of a corporate bond, various subsamples from the bond data base are constructed. The subsamples distinguish between high ratings (ratings AAA and AA) and low ratings (ratings A and BBB) on the one hand and between financial institutions and non-financial corporates on the other. The structural break regression of Equation (3.6) is then estimated for the different subsamples and the parameter estimates for the liquidity proxies are compared. Again, an EGLS approach with firm-level fixed effects is used for the panel regressions. Table 3-6 gives an overview of the different subsamples used in the analysis and reports summary statistics with regard to credit spread changes and changes of relative bid-ask spreads within the different subsamples.

As a first step the effect of illiquidity on credit spread changes before and after the start of the financial crisis is compared with only one differentiating category. Thus, high-rated bonds (subsample I) are compared with low-rated bonds (subsample II) and bonds of financial institutions (subsample A) with bonds of non-financial corporates (subsample B), while the respective other differentiating category (rating or sector) is not regarded.

Table 3-7 reports the regression results with regard to the bond-specific liquidity measure (change of the relative bid-ask spread) and the market-wide liquidity measure (change of the swap spread).[27] Similar to the interpretation of the liquidity impact during the financial crisis on the whole bond sample the pre-crisis parameter estimates (ΔBAS_t and $\Delta Swap_t$) are compared with the post-crisis parameter estimates ($DT^*\Delta BAS_t$ and $DT^*\Delta Swap_t$).

The results clearly indicate that the high-rated bonds in subsample I have been affected more severely from illiquidity during the financial crisis than the low-rated bonds in subsample II.

For high-rated bonds, bond-specific illiquidity was almost irrelevant before the financial crisis (insignificant coefficient for ΔBAS_t close to 0). During the crisis, the impact of bid-ask spread changes on credit spread changes increased significantly, which shows as a parameter estimate for $DT^*\Delta Swap_t$ of more than 0.31. For low-rated bonds, bond-specific illiquidity was already highly relevant before the start of the crisis (significant coefficient for ΔBAS_t of 0.25) and the additional impact during the crisis is neither large (coefficient for $DT^*\Delta Swap_t$ less than 0.04) nor statistically significant.

---

[27] Tables with parameter estimates for all variables are available upon request.

Table 3-7: Liquidity effect on credit spread changes for different credit quality and different sectors

	I: High Rating			II: Low Rating		
	Estimate		Std. err.	Estimate		Std. err.
Bond-specific						
ΔBAS_t	0.0061		0.0165	0.2528	***	0.0393
$DT*\Delta BAS_t$	0.3054	***	0.0510	0.0381		0.0443
Market-wide						
$\Delta Swap_t$	0.1325	***	0.0245	0.1658	***	0.0449
$DT*\Delta Swap_t$	0.5613	***	0.0949	0.4773	***	0.0664

	A: Financial Institutions			B: Non-Financial Corporates		
	Estimate		Std. err.	Estimate		Std. err.
Bond-specific						
ΔBAS_t	0.0904	***	0.0284	0.2528	***	0.0529
$DT*\Delta BAS_t$	0.2591	***	0.0425	0.0058		0.0582
Market-wide						
$\Delta Swap_t$	0.0890	***	0.0243	0.2981	***	0.0437
$DT*\Delta Swap_t$	0.1902	*	0.0981	0.4740	***	0.0603

This table shows the liquidity-related results of the structural break regression for different subsamples. Four subsamples are constructed: the subsamples I, II, A, and B contain bonds rated AAA or AA, bonds rated A or BBB, bonds of financial institutions, and bonds of non-financial corporates, respectively. The iBoxx rating is used as a bond's rating class and the sector is assigned according to the Sector Level 2 in the iBoxx database. Credit spread changes are regressed against changes of bond-specific and market-wide liquidity and a set of control variables. Similar to the structural break analysis, the time dummy variable DT is included as moderator variable in the panel regression. DT takes a value of 0 for all monthly observations from August 2001 through June 2007 and a value of 1 for July 2007 through June 2009. The model is estimated with an EGLS approach and accounts for firm-level fixed effects. Only the parameter estimates for bond-specific liquidity measured by ΔBAS_t and $DT*\Delta BAS_t$ as well as for market-wide liquidity measured by $\Delta Swap_t$ and $DT*\Delta Swap_t$ are shown. White robust standard errors and associated significance levels are reported. *** (**, *) denotes significant parameters at a 1% (5%, 10%) significance level.

Also the results for market-wide liquidity point in the same direction, although all estimated coefficients are statistically significant. This indicates that market-wide liquidity was important for credit spread changes for both subsamples before and after the start of the financial crisis. Nevertheless, the impact of market-wide liquidity on high-rated bonds increased by more than 400%, from 0.13

(pre-crisis) to approximately 0.70 (post-crisis).[28] In contrast, the coefficient for low-rated bonds only increased by less than 300%, from 0.17 to 0.64.

Next the comparison of bonds issued by financial institutions (subsample A) and bonds issued by non-financial corporates (subsample B) is discussed. It can be concluded that during the financial crisis the effect of bond-specific illiquidity on credit spreads increased significantly for financial institutions. The corresponding parameter for $DT^*\Delta BAS_t$ has an estimate of 0.26 and is highly significant, while the pre-crisis effect expressed by the coefficient for ΔBAS_t is comparably low (0.09). Similar to subsample II containing low-rated bonds, bonds of non-financial corporates were almost not at all additionally affected by liquidity changes during the financial crisis. The coefficient for $DT^*\Delta BAS_t$ is economically and statistically not significant. The pre-crisis effect (ΔBAS_t), however, is statistically significant and the parameter estimate of 0.25 implies that the impact of illiquidity on credit spreads was already relevant before the crisis started.

The additional impact of changes in market-wide liquidity during the crisis is also higher for bonds of financial institutions. The impact increased during the financial crisis by more than 200% (from 0.09 to 0.28) for financial institutions, and only by less than 160% (from 0.30 to 0.77) for non-financial corporates.

In order to gain a further understanding of the liquidity impact on credit spreads with regard to credit quality and sector the bond sample is further differentiated by constructing the following mutually exclusive subsamples. Subsamples I.A, I.B, II.A., and II.B contain high-rated bonds of financial institutions, low-rated bonds of financial institutions, high-rated bonds of non-financial corporates, and low-rated bonds of non-financial corporates, respectively. With this approach, it can be identified whether the increasing sensitivity of credit spread changes to changes in liquidity during the financial crisis is linked more strongly to the credit quality or the sector.[29]

Table 3-8 reports the results for the pre- and post-crisis liquidity effects from a pure rating and a pure sector perspective while controlling for the respective other category. The rating-related effects are analyzed by comparing the parameter estimates horizontally within the rows and the sector-related effects by comparing coefficients vertically within the columns.

---

28 As shown in Equation (3.5), the joint impact of market-wide liquidity during the financial crisis is computed as the sum of the coefficients for $\Delta Swap_t$ and $DT^*\Delta Swap_t$.

29 While the analysis above gives a good indication, there is still a potential bias resulting from overlapping subsamples. For example, the liquidity effect observed for high-rated bonds could rather be linked to the sector, if subsample I contains bonds issued by financial institutions. Specifically, the results are ambiguous if the correlation between sector and bond rating is high.

Table 3-8: Rating and sector perspective on the liquidity effect on credit spreads

	I.A: High rating, financial institutions			II.A: Low rating, financial institutions		
	Estimate		Std. err.	Estimate		Std. err.
Bond-specific						
ΔBAS_t	0.0080		0.0151	0.2027	***	0.0537
$DT*\Delta BAS_t$	0.3216	***	0.0649	0.1531	**	0.0670
Market-wide						
$\Delta Swap_t$	0.1220	***	0.0270	-0.0362		0.0484
$DT*\Delta Swap_t$	0.7657	***	0.1186	-0.1953		0.1746
	I.B: High rating, non-financial corporates			II.B Low rating, non-financial corporates		
	Estimate		Std. err.	Estimate		Std. err.
Bond-specific						
ΔBAS_t	-0.0297		0.0342	0.2891	***	0.0617
$DT*\Delta BAS_t$	0.2448	***	0.0716	-0.0338		0.0663
Market-wide						
$\Delta Swap_t$	0.1381	***	0.0421	0.3423	***	0.0505
$DT*\Delta Swap_t$	0.2291		0.1410	0.4600	***	0.0664

This table shows the liquidity-related results of the structural break regression for different subsamples. Four subsamples are constructed: the subsamples I.A, II.A, I.B, and II.B contain bonds of financial institutions rated AAA or AA, bonds of financial institutions rated A or BBB, bonds of non-financial corporates rated AAA or AA, and bonds of non-financial corporates rated A or BBB, respectively. The iBoxx rating is used as a bond's rating class and the sector is assigned according to the Sector Level 2 in the iBoxx database. Credit spread changes are regressed against changes of bond-specific and market-wide liquidity and a set of control variables. Similar to the structural break analysis, the time dummy variable DT is included as moderator variable in the panel regression. DT takes a value of 0 for all monthly observations from August 2001 through June 2007 and a value of 1 for July 2007 through June 2009. The model is estimated with an EGLS approach and accounts for firm-level fixed effects. Only the parameter estimates for bond-specific liquidity measured by ΔBAS_t and $DT*\Delta BAS_t$ as well as for market-wide liquidity measured by $\Delta Swap_t$ and $DT*\Delta Swap_t$ are shown. White robust standard errors and associated significance levels are reported. *** (**, *) denotes significant parameters at a 1% (5%, 10%) significance level.

First, high-rated bonds are compared with low-rated bonds within the two disjunct sectors. The result for the effect of bond-specific illiquidity during the financial crisis is unambiguous. For the two subsamples containing low-rated bonds (II.A and II.B), all estimates for $DT*\Delta BAS_t$ are lower than the estimates for ΔBAS_t or they are not significant. In contrast, for the subsamples of high-rated bonds (I.A and I.B), the post-crisis coefficients for bond-specific liquidity are larger than the pre-crisis coefficients and they are highly significant. Thus, it can be concluded that, irrespective of the sector, high-rated bonds have been affected more severely from a dry-up in bond-specific liquidity during the financial crisis than in the pre-crisis period.

Market-wide illiquidity has hit high-rated bonds of financial institutions more strongly than low-rated bonds within that sector.[30] For high-rated bonds of non-financial corporates the impact of market-wide illiquidity has risen by 166% (from 0.14 to 0.37) during the financial crisis compared to 134% (from 0.34 to 0.80) for low-rated bonds of non-financial corporates. However, the effect for high-rated corporates is not significant because the estimate for $DT^*\Delta Swap_t$ (0.23) is statistically insignificant at conventional significance levels.

Second, the sector perspective is regarded where bonds of financial institutions are compared with bonds of non-financial corporates within the two disjunct rating categories.[31] Again, the result for the effect of changes in bond-specific liquidity is unambiguous. Comparing the parameter estimates of the two subsamples containing low-rated bonds (II.A and II.B), the post-crisis estimate of the additional impact of changes in the bid-ask spread is not significant for non-financial corporates (-0.03), whereas the estimate for bonds of financial institutions is positive (0.15) and statistically significant. Within the two subsamples of high-rated bonds (I.A and I.B) both estimates for $DT^*\Delta BAS_t$ are positive and significant and both estimates for ΔBAS_t are statistically insignificant. Therefore, the pre-crisis effect of bond-specific liquidity on credit spreads is not measurable and the absolute increase during the post-crisis period can be compared, which is higher for bonds of financial institutions (0.32) than for bonds of non-financial corporates (0.24). Thus, it can be concluded that, irrespective of the credit quality, bonds of financial institutions have been affected more severely from a dry-up in bond-specific liquidity during the financial crisis than in the pre-crisis period.

As observed for the rating perspective the effect of market-wide liquidity is ambiguous for the sector perspective, too. The results show that within the subsamples of high-rated bonds, bonds of financial institutions were hit more strongly than bonds of corporates from declining market-wide liquidity during the financial crisis. The corresponding coefficients for $DT^*\Delta Swap_t$ are very high (0.77) and significant for financial institutions and comparably low (0.22) and

---

30 In fact, for low-rated bonds of financial institutions changes in market-wide liquidity have no significant impact at all.
31 That means, the parameter estimates in Table 3-8 are compared vertically.

insignificant for corporates. The results are different for low-rated bonds. Here, a significant increase of the post-crisis effect of market-wide liquidity for non-financial corporates can be observed. For low-rated bonds of financial institutions, changes in market-wide liquidity do not have a significant impact on credit spreads changes neither before nor after the start of the financial crisis.

3.4.4 Summary of Empirical Analyses

The basis regression confirms existing theoretical and empirical findings that changes in bond-specific and market-wide liquidity have a significant impact on credit spread changes. Based on the structural break analysis the conclusion is drawn that liquidity has become much more relevant in explaining credit spread changes during the recent financial crisis. A comparison of the results from structural break regressions with different subsamples gives additional insights into the effect of the financial crisis on different credit qualities and sectors. Overall, high-rated bonds and bonds of financial institutions have a higher exposure to liquidity risk during the financial crisis compared to low-rated bonds and bonds of non-financial corporates. While this result is unambiguously true for bond-specific liquidity, there are deviations from this general finding for the effects of market-wide liquidity. Here, high-rated bonds of financial institutions and low-rated bonds of non-financial corporates exhibit the strongest sensitivity to rising market-wide illiquidity during the financial crisis.

3.5 Conclusion

Theoretical and empirical literature has identified liquidity as a risk driver for prices and spreads of corporate bonds and the results of this study confirm these findings for the European corporate bond market. However, the impact of the financial crisis on the relationship between liquidity and credit spreads has not been regarded before.

This paper closes that gap by analyzing the effects of the financial crisis with a structural break approach. It conducts a panel regression on a sample of European corporate bonds, accounting for bond-specific heteroscedasticity and firm-level fixed effects. Controlling for a set of theoretical determinants of credit spreads, the study finds that the risk of bond-specific and market-wide illiquidity has a significantly larger impact on credit spreads during the financial crisis compared to the pre-crisis period. In contrast, a significant impact of typical variables measuring credit risk, such as rating migration and leverage deterioration, cannot be confirmed.

Furthermore, it is shown that high-rated bonds and bonds of financial institutions have been affected more strongly by illiquidity during the financial crisis than low-rated bonds and bonds of non-financial corporates. This result is especially interesting against the background of the existing regulatory framework for banks. The Basel II accord in its pre-crisis version required banks to hold comparably little capital for market risks arising from bonds with a good credit quality. Liquidity risk was thus underrepresented in regulatory frameworks and banks' risk management at the onset of the financial crisis. This was especially revealed by massive write-offs in the banking sector that brought several banks to the brink of bankruptcy. In this regard this study supports the call for a revised banking regulation that attaches more importance to liquidity risk, particularly for asset classes with little credit risk.

4 Study 3: The Short and Long-Term Determinants of Credit Spreads – An Analysis for the European Corporate Bond Market

4.1 Introduction

During the financial crisis 2007/2008 the pricing of corporate debt and credit derivatives gained a renewed importance and standard regression approaches failed to explain the highly volatile credit spreads. Recent European evidence also indicates that credit spreads are closely linked to economic variables such as the yield curve, market liquidity, or the equity market. Furthermore, credit spreads and most of their theoretical determinants exhibit non-stationary characteristics for the overall period where reliable data is available for the European corporate bond market.

Theory provides two different approaches to price risky debt. Structural models use option pricing theory to price debt as a combination of a risk-free asset and an option on the firm value (e.g., Merton (1974), Leland (1994), Longstaff and Schwartz (1995), Collin-Dufresne and Goldstein (2001)). In contrast, reduced-form approaches model the default event based on the occurrence of default and the recovery rate in case of a default (e.g., Jarrow and Turnbull (1995), Duffie and Singleton (1999)).

Both types of model have been extensively tested in empirical studies of credit spreads mainly for the U.S. corporate bond market and findings indicate that credit spread variations are only partially explained by observable variables (see e.g., Duffee (1998), Collin-Dufresne *et al.* (2001), Chen *et al.* (2007)). However, almost all empirical studies of credit spreads concentrate on the short-term relationship by regressing credit spread changes on a set of determining variables. First differences are used to avoid spurious results that arise if level data of the time series are not stationary (e.g., Longstaff and Schwartz (1995), Duffee (1998), Collin-Dufresne *et al.* (2001)). Thus, they mainly analyze the short-term dynamics of credit spreads while neglecting information about possible long-term relationships between the variables, which are captured by the levels of the time series. If a long-term equilibrium exists between credit spreads and their determinants, cointegration analysis is a more appropriate approach, since it includes both the long-term relationship between the variables and the short-term adjustment processes. In addition, if the variables are linked by cointegration relationships, regression models that omit the long-term relationship could be biased according to Duan and Pliska (2004).

Following these arguments this study analyzes credit spread variations with a cointegration approach. Cointegration analysis has the merit of simultaneously detecting a long-term relationship between the endogenous variables and estimating the short-term dynamics of the adjustment process towards the equilibrium relationship. Thus, it can be tested if the theoretical determinants have the predicted impact on credit spreads in the long-run and if disequilibriums converge back to the long-term equilibrium.

This study extends existing research in three important ways. First, it disentangles the long-term and the short-term influences of a broad range of determinants and analyzes the simultaneous interactions between the endogenous variables. Besides the usually included risk-free rate, the complete term structure, the return and the volatility of the equity market, a liquidity factor, and the inflation rate are incorporated. In contrast, previous studies mainly examined the partial relations between credit spreads and a few selected factors. Second, this study conducts an analysis for the European corporate bond market and the sample includes the recent financial crisis. With that dataset, the empirical evidence is considerably extended both on the geographical and the time dimension. Third, the recently developed ARDL approach to cointegration is applied as a robustness check to the results of the Johansen cointegration test in order to derive reliable estimates for the long-term and short-term dynamics of credit spreads.

The results confirm the theoretically predicted long-run interdependencies between credit spreads and their determinants. For both cointegration techniques, strong evidence for the existence of a long-term relationship between credit spreads and their relevant factors is found. The error correction model (ECM) shows a significant error correction term between -30% and -40% and is able to explain more than 80% of credit spread variations according to the ARDL approach.

Comparing actual credit spreads with equilibrium credit spreads that result from the estimated long-term relationship the study furthermore identifies a strong over-pricing of credit spreads in the aftermath of the collapse of Lehman Brothers. Only at the end of 2009 a convergence of credit spreads towards equilibrium can be observed.

The remainder of this paper is organized as follows. In the next section the existing literature on credit spread models is discussed to develop the theoretical and empirical background for the study. Section 4.3 provides an overview of the methodology of the analyses regarding the Johansen and the ARDL cointegration approaches. Section 4.4 describes the data that is used for the subsequent empirical analysis. In Section 4.5 the empirical results of the two cointegration approaches are discussed. Section 4.6 gives the conclusions.

4.2 Theoretical Background and Related Literature

4.2.1 Determinants of Credit Spreads

Structural models of default risk, introduced by Merton (1974), build on the option pricing model developed by Black and Scholes (1973). The underlying principle of this class of model is that equity can be seen as a contingent claim on the firm's assets and corporate debt is priced as combination of a risk-free bond and a short position in a put on the firm's assets. Hence, structural models include the risk-free rate, the firm's leverage as a proxy for the asset value, and equity volatility as main determinants of credit spreads.

In most structural models, the risk-free rate is assumed to be negatively related to credit spreads, which is also supported by empirical evidence (see e.g., Collin-Dufresne *et al.* (2001), Chen *et al.* (2007)). Longstaff and Schwartz (1995) propose that the risk-neutral drift of the firm value process increases with a rising spot rate with the effect of a declining probability of default and an increasing firm value. Consequently, the value of a put option on the firm's assets is reduced and the short position in the put option increases in value. As a result, the value of the corporate bond increases and the credit spread tightens if the risk-free rate rises.

In structural models, the leverage is positively related to the default risk of a firm. Increasing leverage ratios lead to increasing default probabilities and hence widening credit spreads. According to Davies (2008), the leverage effect can be approximated by the overall equity market if aggregate models are applied. In line with Ericsson and Renault (2006), increasing market returns are associated with a deleveraging of firms with the result of decreasing default probabilities and credit spreads.

According to option pricing theory, increasing equity volatility leads to increasing option values. Since structural models link the bond price to a short position in a put option on the firm value, increasing volatility should lead to decreasing bond prices and increasing credit spreads.

Other models extend the early structural models by including further variables that could determine corporate credit spreads. Duffee (1998) or Collin-Dufresne *et al.* (2001), for example, argue that not only the level but also the slope and the convexity of the risk-free yield curve are relevant to explain credit spreads.

Collin-Dufresne et al. (2001) propose a negative relation between the slope of the risk-free yield curve and credit spreads. They claim that an increasing slope of the yield curve expresses the expectation of rising interest rates in the future, which reduces credit spreads based on the same arguments discussed above.

More recent studies also include a liquidity factor to explain credit spreads in order to account for the fact that corporate bond markets are less liquid than government bond markets and that investors demand yield premiums for holding illiquid assets.[32] Longstaff et al. (2005) argue that market-wide illiquidity of bonds often results from a flight to quality with the effect that corporate bonds trade at a discount compared to highly liquid Treasury bonds. Thus, illiquidity in the corporate bond market leads to lower bond prices and higher credit spreads.

Finally, macroeconomic factors such as the inflation rate can explain credit spread deviations. Athanassakos and Carayannopoulos (2001), for example, propose that inflation should be positively related to credit spreads because risk premiums for corporate bond investments rise during periods of high inflation.

Based on these findings, this study tests the relationship between credit spreads (CS) and their theoretical determinants according to the following equation:

$$CS = f(Term, Equity, Liquidity, Macro), \qquad (4.1)$$

where *Term* includes parameters of the term structure of the risk-free interest rate, such as level, slope, and convexity of the yield curve; *Equity* represents equity market factors, such as the stock market return and the stock market volatility; *Liquidity* stands for corporate bond market liquidity; and *Macro* includes macroeconomic factors, such as the inflation rate. With the choice of this broad range of factors, the study considerably extends existing cointegration analyses of credit spreads, which are summarized in the following section.

4.2.2 Cointegration Analyses of Credit Spreads

A few studies have conducted cointegration analyses of credit spreads for the U.S. corporate bond market. Neal et al. (2000) find a cointegration relationship between corporate credit spreads and government bond rates using a Johansen approach. They also conduct a robustness check of their results with an Engle and Granger (1987) cointegration test. Overall, they find a negative relationship between Treasury rates and credit spread in the short-run as well as a positive relationship in the long-run, which implies that the correlation between interest

---

32 See, e.g., Ericsson and Renault (2006), Collin-Dufresne et al. (2001), or Longstaff et al. (2005).

rates and credit spreads is time-varying and not constant, as most theoretical models predict.

Using Johansen tests, Joutz *et al.* (2001) conduct a cointegration analysis for the relationship between credit spreads and level and slope of the risk-free yield curve. Furthermore, they include Fama and French (1993) factors as unrestricted variables. The findings support the existence of a long-run relationship between the endogenous variables, but the relationship between credit spreads and the term structure variables varies with different maturities and credit qualities.

Pape and Schlecker (2007) use an Engle and Granger (1987) cointegration approach to test the long-term relationship between different measures of credit spreads and spread determinants such as the risk-free interest rate, a stock market index, and the spread between the swap curve and the Treasury yield curve. Credit spreads are negatively related to the risk-free rate and the stock market index; however, they are positively related to the swap spread.

Miloudi and Moraux (2009) apply a Johansen cointegration approach to analyze the long-term relationship between credit spreads, the level and the slope of the risk-free yield curve, and the stock market. They find support for a positive relationship between the level of the yield curve and credit spreads and a negative relationship between the slope of the yield curve and credit spreads as well as between the stock market and credit spreads.

Davies (2008) also uses a Johansen cointegration approach and tests the long-term relationship between credit spreads, the risk-free rate, the stock market, and industrial production. In addition, he includes the stationary slope of the Treasury curve as further exogenous variable. In contrast to common theory, he reports that credit spreads are positively related to the risk-free rate and the stock market in the long-run. Furthermore, there is a negative long-run relationship between credit spreads and industrial production.

In the context of the cointegration analysis, Equation (4.1) is defined as the long-term relationship between credit spreads and their determinants. The short-term dynamics of credit spreads are then analyzed based on an ECM. The long-term and short-term dynamics are estimated with both, the Johansen and the ARDL approach.

4.3 Cointegration Tests

Cointegration analysis requires the endogenous variables to be integrated or at least nearly integrated. While all variables need to be purely I(1) in the Johansen cointegration approach, the ARDL cointegration procedure relaxes these strict assumptions because a mix of I(0) and I(1) variables is allowed. Nevertheless, for the ARDL approach it has to be ensured that none of the variables is I(2).

Therefore, two different unit root tests are conducted in order to determine the order of integration of the time series. First, ADF unit root tests are applied. However, since the ADF test does not yield stable results in presence of a structural break in the time series and it cannot be ruled out that the financial crisis represents a structural break, a second unit root test developed by Zivot and Andrews (1992), hereafter ZA, is applied. According to ZA, the results of conventional unit root tests may be reversed if the time of a structural break is endogenously determined.

The multivariate cointegration analysis of Johansen (1991) assumes that there may be more than one cointegration relation between several endogenous I(1) variables. The cointegration test is based on the following vector error correction equation:

$$\Delta z_t = \Pi z_{t-1} + \sum_{i=1}^{p} \Gamma_i \Delta z_{t-i} + B w_t + \varepsilon_t, \tag{4.2}$$

where z_t is a k-dimensional vector of non-stationary I(1) variables, w_t is a vector of deterministic variables, and the residuals ε_t are white noise. If the matrix Π has a reduced rank of r ($0 < r < k$), it can be expressed as

$$\Pi = \alpha \beta', \tag{4.3}$$

so that the linear combinations $\beta' z_t$ are stationary. The columns of the $r \times k$ matrix β contain the r cointegrating vectors and the elements of α are the adjustment parameters of the vector error correction model (VECM) in Equation (4.2). Johansen (1991) proposes to estimate the cointegration vectors with a maximum likelihood method. His approach starts by estimating the matrix Π from an unrestricted VAR model. Then, he suggests to test whether the restrictions from a reduced rank of Π can be rejected based on the number of significant eigenvalues of the estimated matrix Π. This is done sequentially from $r = 0$ to $r = k-1$ until one fails to reject the null hypothesis of r cointegration relations.

There are two procedures to test the significance of the eigenvalues of Π. The trace statistic LR_{tr} tests the null of r cointegration relations against the alternative of a stationary VAR, i.e. k cointegration relations:

$$LR_{tr}(r \mid k) = -T \sum_{i=r+1}^{k} \log(1 - \lambda_i), \tag{4.4}$$

where T is the number of observations and λ_i is the i-th largest eigenvalue of Π.

The maximum eigenvalue statistic LR_{me} tests the null of r cointegration relations against the alternative of $r+1$ cointegration relations:

$$LR_{me}(r \mid r+1) = -T \log(1 - \lambda_{r+1}). \tag{4.5}$$

After determining the existence and the number of cointegration relations between the endogenous variables z_t, the VECM in Equation (4.2) can be estimated because all elements entering the VECM are stationary. The parameters of matrix α determine the speed of short-term adjustments towards the long-term relationship between the cointegrated variables.

In addition to the Johansen cointegration approach the ARDL cointegration procedure developed by Pesaran and Shin (1999) and Pesaran et al. (2001) is applied to further validate the results. The advantage of using an ARDL approach is that the variables are not required to be purely I(1), cointegration can also be tested for co-existing I(0) and I(1) variables. In contrast to the Johansen approach, it is applicable irrespective of whether the variables entering the model are purely I(0), purely I(1), or a mix of I(0) and I(1). Furthermore, the ARDL cointegration approach uses OLS instead of maximum likelihood. The former estimation technique is more efficient in small samples cases and the setup is more flexible in modeling the dynamics of the variables. Because of these advantages, empirical literature using the ARDL procedure has steadily grown in recent years.

The ARDL cointegration approach starts by estimating the following unrestricted error correction model (UECM) by OLS:

$$\Delta y_t = \delta_0 y_{t-1} + \sum_{i=1}^{k} \delta_i x_{i,t-1} + \sum_{i=1}^{p-1} \tau_i \Delta y_{t-i} + \sum_{i=1}^{k}\sum_{j=0}^{p-1} \phi_{i,j} \Delta x_{i,t-j} + \gamma' w_t + \varepsilon_t, \tag{4.6}$$

where y_t is the dependent variable, k is the number of forcing variables $x_{i,t}$, and w_t is a vector of deterministic variables such as intercept, dummy variables or trends. In the UECM the lag length p is the same for the dependent variable and the forcing variables.

To test whether a long-term relationship exists between y_t and the forcing variables $x_{i,t}$ Pesaran et al. (2001) propose to use a bounds testing procedure by conducting a Wald test for the joint significance of the lagged levels of the variables in Equation (4.6). Specifically, the null of $\delta_0 = \delta_1 = \delta_2 = ... = \delta_k = 0$ is tested against the alternative that the parameters are jointly significant, i.e. that at least one δ_i, for all i ($i = 0, 1, 2, ..., k$), is different from zero. The asymptotic distribution of the resulting F-statistic is, however, non-standard under the null hypothesis that no long-term relationship between the variables exists. Pesaran et al. (2001) provide two sets of asymptotic critical value bounds. If the computed

F-statistic is below the lower bound, all variables are purely I(0) and the null hypothesis of no long-term relationship cannot be rejected. On the other hand, if the computed F-statistic exceeds the upper bound, all variables are assumed to be purely I(1) and the null hypothesis of no long-term relationship has to be rejected. In both cases a conclusive inference can be made irrespective of the integration status of the variables. If the computed F-statistic falls within the lower and the upper bound, the inference is inconclusive and one has to know the true order of integration of the underlying variables.

In addition to the Wald test of joint significance of the lagged variables, Pesaran *et al.* (2001) propose another bounds test that relates to the cointegration test of Banerjee *et al.* (1998). This test is based on the t-statistic of the lagged dependent variable in Equation (4.6), i.e. the t-value of δ_0 is tested against an upper and a lower critical value bound. The inference to the existence of a long-run relationship is the same as described above for the Wald test.

Once cointegration has been established, Pesaran *et al.* (2001) propose to estimate a conditional ARDL model by OLS:

$$y_t = \sum_{i=1}^{p} \varphi_i y_{t-i} + \sum_{i=1}^{k} \sum_{j=0}^{q_i} \beta_{i,j} x_{i,t-j} + \eta' w_t + \xi_t, \qquad (4.7)$$

where y_t, x_t, and w_t are as previously defined. In contrast to the common lag length in the UECM of Equation (4.6), the number of lags p and q_i, for all i ($i = 1, 2, \ldots, k$), in Equation (4.7) may vary for the different variables. After the maximum number of lags is defined, the approach selects the optimal lag length for each variable based on an information criterion, such as the Schwarz information criterion (SIC) or the Akaike information criterion (AIC). This procedure involves estimating all possible ARDL models in Equation (4.7), i.e. a total of $(m+1)^{k+1}$ different regressions, where m is the maximum lag order for p and all q_i. Then the lag distribution that optimizes the chosen information criterion is used for the subsequent analyses.[33]

Based on the estimated ARDL $(\hat{p}, \hat{q}_1, \hat{q}_2, \ldots, \hat{q}_k)$ model in Equation (4.7), the long-term relationship between y_t and the forcing variables $x_{i,t}$ can be expressed as:

$$y_t = \sum_{i=1}^{k} \hat{\theta}_i x_{i,t} + \hat{\psi}' w_t, \qquad (4.8)$$

---

[33] See Pesaran and Pesaran (2009) for a detailed description of the ARDL approach and a derivation of the required formulae.

where the long-run coefficients are calculated as:

$$\hat{\theta}_i = \frac{\sum_{j=0}^{\hat{q}_i}\hat{\beta}_{i,j}}{1-\sum_{j=1}^{\hat{p}}\hat{\phi}_j} \quad \text{and} \quad \hat{\psi} = \frac{\hat{\eta}}{1-\sum_{j=1}^{\hat{p}}\hat{\phi}_j}. \quad (4.9)$$

Finally, a conditional ECM associated with the ARDL $(\hat{p},\hat{q}_1,\hat{q}_2,...,\hat{q}_k)$ model can be obtained by transforming Equation (4.7) into first differences:

$$\Delta y_t = \lambda EC_{t-1} + \sum_{i=1}^{\hat{p}-1}\varphi_i^*\Delta y_{t-i} + \sum_{i=1}^{k}\sum_{j=0}^{\hat{q}_i-1}\beta_{i,j}^*\Delta x_{i,t-j} + \eta'\Delta w_t + \xi_t, \quad (4.10)$$

where λ is the adjustment parameter expressing the strength with which the ECM adjusts to deviations from the long-term relationship between the cointegrated variables. The error correction term EC_t is defined as:

$$EC_t = y_t - \sum_{i=1}^{k}\hat{\theta}_i x_{i,t} - \hat{\psi}'w_t. \quad (4.11)$$

4.4 Data

The data sample includes 132 data points of monthly observations from January 1999 through December 2009 and the variables relate to the European corporate bond market. The start of the EMU in January 1999 marks the earliest possible date where a European-wide analysis is meaningful. Table 4-1 shows summary statistics of the variables used in the model and Figure 4-1 depicts the time series of the variables.

Table 4-1: Summary statistics of variables

	CS_t	$Level_t$	$Slope_t$	$Convex_t$	Ret_t	$Vola_t$	$Swap_t$	CPI_t
Mean	0.0123	0.0308	0.0099	0.0328	-0.0190	0.2607	0.0024	0.0178
Max	0.0485	0.0515	0.0220	0.0521	0.3971	0.6327	0.0070	0.0306
Min	0.0043	0.0069	-0.0002	0.0138	-0.6337	0.1264	0.0006	0.0071
Std. dev.	0.0098	0.0111	0.0061	0.0097	0.2674	0.1047	0.0015	0.0058
Skewness	2.3826	-0.2276	0.0828	-0.0531	-0.5812	1.2691	0.9832	-0.0629
Kurtosis	8.3431	2.3105	1.9716	2.1194	2.2562	4.4709	3.3598	2.1678

This table reports the summary statistics for the endogenous variables of the cointegration analysis. The sample includes 132 monthly observations from January 1999 through December 2009.

Credit spreads (CS_t) are calculated as differences between the average annual yields to maturity of the *iBoxx Corporates Index* of euro-denominated bonds and the yields to maturity of corresponding government bonds. The latter are obtained from Bloomberg data on the fair market curve of AAA-rated EU government bonds with a time to maturity that matches the average time to maturity of the *iBoxx Corporates Index* in the respective month.

Next, data on the term structure of the risk-free yield curve is used. All risk-free yields are taken from Bloomberg data on the fair market yield curves of AAA-rated EU government bonds. First, the monthly average of the one-year risk-free yield is used as proxy for the level of the yield curve ($Level_t$). Second, in line with Chen et al. (2007) and Collin-Dufresne et al. (2001), the slope of the yield curve ($Slope_t$) is calculated as the difference between the average ten-year risk-free yield and the average two-year risk-free yield. Third, the difference between the five-year and the average of the ten-year and the two-year risk-free yields is used to approximate the convexity of the yield curve ($Convex_t$). This approach is suggested, for example, by Castagnetti and Rossi (2008).

The equity market return (Ret_t) is measured as the year-on-year return of the *EuroStoxx50* stock market index and the implied volatility index of the *EuroStoxx50* is used to represent stock market volatility ($Vola_t$).[34] Both time series are obtained from Thomson Reuters Datastream.

---

[34] The use of equity indices and implied volatility indices to measure equity returns and equity volatility, respectively, is used in many credit spread studies, such as Ericsson and Renault (2006), Collin-Dufresne et al. (2001) or Van Landschoot (2008), among others.

Figure 4-1: Time series of variables

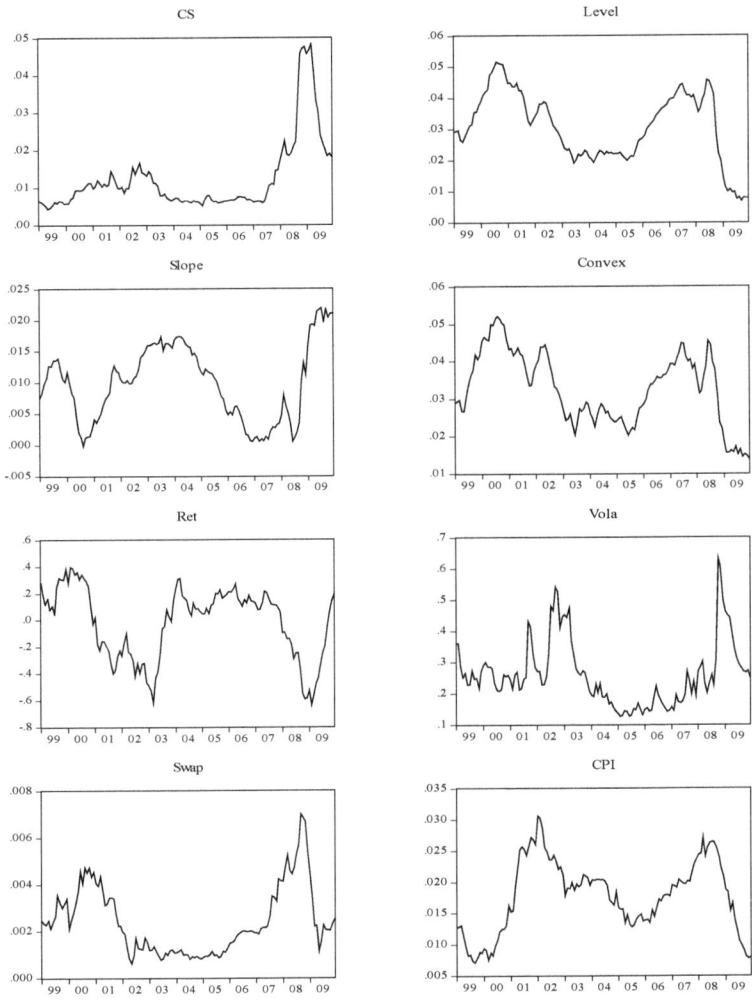

This figure shows the time series of the endogenous variables during the sample period of January 1999-December 2009.

Following Collin-Dufresne *et al.* (2001) or Castagnetti and Rossi (2008), the difference between the five-year euro swap rate and the five-year government bond yield is used as proxy for liquidity in the corporate bond market ($SWAP_t$). Both time series are taken from Bloomberg. According to Collin-Dufresne et al. (2001) swap market liquidity and corporate bond market liquidity are strongly interlinked and Castagnetti and Rossi (2008) argue that this is because issuers of corporate bonds typically fund on the swap market. Therefore, rising swap spreads are assumed to indicate a decreasing liquidity in the corporate bond market due to the investors' preference for less risky government bonds.

Inflation (CPI_t) is measured as the annual growth rate of the *harmonized consumer price index excluding energy* published by the ECB. The growth rate is calculated as twelve-month log differences of end-of-month observations of the index.

Finally, a dummy variable (D_{crisis}) is included for the months where the effect of the recent financial crisis was most evident in the variation of credit spreads. The time span of the peak of the financial crisis is determined from the credit spread time series. The dummy variable takes a value of 1 for those observations where credit spreads were more than two standard deviations above the overall average of 123 basis points and a value of 0 elsewhere. Based on this method a range from September 2008 through May 2009 is obtained for the peak of the financial crisis. The start of this endogenously estimated period coincides with the collapse of the investment bank Lehman Brothers and the period lasts through the first months of the year 2009, where many banks announced their 2008 losses caused by huge write-offs of toxic assets.

4.5 Empirical Results of Credit Spread Dynamics

This section discusses the parameter estimates that are derived from the two cointegration approaches. In doing so, the existence of a long-term relationship is tested and the short-term dynamics between credit spreads and their determinants are estimated. The long-term relationship can be expressed as a linear function of credit spreads:

$$CS_t = c_0 + c_1 Level_t + c_2 Slope_t + c_3 Convex_t + c_4 R\,et_t + c_5 Vola_t \\ + c_6 Swap_t + c_7 CPI_t + \varepsilon_t \qquad (4.12)$$

Table 4-2 summarizes the expected long-term effects of the determinants on credit spreads based on the theoretical discussion in Section 4.2.1.

Table 4-2: Expected long-term effects of determining variables on credit spreads

Determinant	Variable	Expected long-term effect on credit spreads	Economic rationale
Risk-free interest rate	$Level_t$	Negative	A higher risk-free rate increases the risk-neutral drift of the firm value process and reduces the probability of default.
Slope of the yield curve	$Slope_t$	Negative	An increasing slope of the yield curve reflects the expectation of a higher interest rate in the future.
Convexity of the yield curve	$Convex_t$	Ambiguous	No clear theoretical prediction.
Stock market return	Ret_t	Negative	High stock market returns indicate deleveraging of firms and decreasing default probabilities.
Stock market volatility	$Vola_t$	Positive	Option prices rise with increasing volatility leading to decreasing bond prices in structural models.
Corporate bond market illiquidity	$Swap_t$	Positive	A rising swap rate indicates a preference for less risky Treasury bonds and decreasing liquidity in the corporate bond market, which is closely linked to the swap market. Since investors demand premiums for holding illiquid assets, increasing market-wide illiquidity leads to decreasing bond prices.
Inflation	CPI_t	Positive	Investors demand risk premiums in times of high inflation.

This table outlines the expected long-term effects of the (forcing) variables on credit spreads based on theoretical considerations.

Some of the variables are considered stationary in existing literature, such as interest rates. While this is most probably true for long observation periods, this study finds evidence for non-stationarity of the variables during the time period under consideration. In line with the arguments of Neal *et al.* (2000), the finite sample evidence of the data, which indicates that the processes are non-stationary, is used in order to conduct statistical inference.

The results of the ADF unit root tests for the endogenous variables (see Table 4-3) suggest that the null of non-stationary level data cannot be rejected for any of the variables at a 5% level – irrespective of whether a constant, a constant and a trend, or neither constant nor trend are included in the test equation. Only at a 10% level non-stationarity would be rejected for levels of $Vola_t$ and Ret_t. The existence of unit roots in the first differences of all variables is strongly rejected at a 1% level. Hence, it is concluded from the ADF unit root tests that all variables are I(1).

Table 4-3: Augmented Dickey-Fuller unit root tests

	Level data									
	Constant, trend				Constant				None	
	t-stat	p	Prob		t-stat	p	Prob		t-stat	p	Prob
CS_t	-2.52	1	0.32	-2.17	1	0.22	-1.12		1	0.24
$Level_t$	-1.85	1	0.67	-1.37	1	0.59	-0.93		1	0.31
$Slope_t$	-2.08	3	0.55	-2.10	3	0.24	-0.82		3	0.36
$Convex_t$	-2.29	1	0.44	-1.61	1	0.47	-0.84		1	0.35
Ret_t	-1.53	0	0.81	-1.75	0	0.41	-1.74	*	0	0.08
$Vola_t$	-2.82	0	0.19	-2.84	*	0	0.06	-1.22		0	0.20
$Swap_t$	-1.93	1	0.63	-1.93	1	0.32	-0.94		1	0.31
CPI_t	-2.33	12	0.41	-2.48	12	0.12	-0.40		12	0.54

	First differences		
	Constant, trend		
	t-stat		p	Prob
CS_t	-6.75	***	0	0.00
$Level_t$	-6.44	***	0	0.00
$Slope_t$	-8.66	***	0	0.00
$Convex_t$	-7.40	***	0	0.00
Ret_t	-9.91	***	0	0.00
$Vola_t$	-10.12	***	0	0.00
$Swap_t$	-9.57	***	0	0.00
CPI_t	-4.04	***	11	0.01

This table shows the results of ADF unit root tests for the endogenous variables of the cointegration analysis. A maximum of twelve lags is assumed and the lag length p is chosen based on the SIC. The reported probabilities are MacKinnon (1996) one-sided p-values. *** (**, *) denotes a rejection of the null of a unit root at a 1% (5%, 10%) significance level.

Furthermore, ZA unit root tests are conduced to double-check the results of the ADF tests under the assumption of one endogenous structural break in the individual time series. The results are reported in Table 4.4. Irrespective of the test specification the null of non-stationary level data cannot be rejected for any of the variables at a 1% level.

For higher significance levels there are some exceptions. At a 5% level, levels of CS_t are assumed to be stationary if the specification that includes only an intercept is used. In addition, at a 10% level, levels of $Vola_t$ are assumed to be stationary if the specification that includes only an intercept or the specification that includes an intercept and a trend in the test equation is used. For all other variables the existence of unit roots in level data cannot be rejected at a 10% level. Non-stationarity in the first differences of all variables is rejected at a 5% level if the most flexible specification (with intercept and trend) is used.[35]

Table 4-4: Zivot-Andrews unit root tests

	Level data						
	Model A			Model B		Model C	
	t-stat		Break	t-stat	Break	t-stat	Break
CS_t	-5.07	**	2008M05	-3.87	2006M09	-4.28	2008M05
$Level_t$	-3.27		2005M10	-2.49	2008M05	-3.37	2006M03
$Slope_t$	-2.83		2005M05	-2.59	2008M04	-3.12	2005M07
$Convex_t$	-3.51		2005M10	-2.70	2008M04	-3.56	2005M10
Ret_t	-3.18		2004M06	-2.24	2006M09	-3.20	2003M04
$Vola_t$	-4.63	*	2003M04	-3.58	2006M03	-4.83 *	2003M04
$Swap_t$	-3.47		2001M10	-3.16	2003M06	-3.38	2001M10
CPI_t	-2.82		2000M12	-2.80	2001M04	-2.84	2001M03

	First differences		
	Model C		
	t-stat		Break
CS_t	-7.49	***	2007M11
$Level_t$	-5.75	***	2003M07
$Slope_t$	-5.39	**	2004M04
$Convex_t$	-6.38	***	2003M07
Ret_t	-5.62	***	2002M10
$Vola_t$	-9.23	***	2002M10
$Swap_t$	-6.81	***	2002M06
CPI_t	-7.69	***	2001M06

This table shows the results of ZA unit root tests with one endogenous structural break for the endogenous variables of the cointegration analysis. A maximum of twelve lags is assumed and the lag length is chosen based on the AIC. Three different models are tested for the level data: A includes only an intercept, B includes only a trend, and C includes an intercept and a trend in the test equation. Asymptotic critical values are: -5.34 (-4.80, -4.58) for the 1% (5%, 10%) level for model A; -4.93 (-4.42, -4.11) for the 1% (5%, 10%) level for model B; and -5.57 (-5.08, -4.82) for the 1% (5%, 10%) level for model C. *** (**, *) denotes a rejection of the null of a unit root at a 1% (5%, 10%) significance level. The break dates are endogenously determined by running the test equations sequentially.

---

35 Unit roots in differenced data are even rejected at a 1% level for all variables except $Slope_t$.

Based on the results of the two different unit root tests all variables are assumed to be I(1) for the following Johansen cointegration approach as only little evidence for stationarity of level data of CS_t and $Vola_t$ is found. It is also concluded from both unit root tests that none of the variables are I(2) because differenced data of all variables are presumed to be stationary at conventional levels of significance. Hence, the prerequisites for OLS estimation in the ARDL approach are given.

4.5.1 Results of Johansen Cointegration Test

Having established that the endogenous variables are all I(1) this section proceeds with the discussion of the results from the Johansen cointegration approach.

The Johansen cointegration test requires certain assumptions with regard to the test specification. In Equation (4.2) the vector z_t contains the endogenous variables CS_t, $Level_t$, $Slope_t$, $Convex_t$, Ret_t, $Vola_t$, $SWAP_t$, and CPI_t; w_t includes the exogenous financial crisis dummy variable D_{crisis}. As the variables do not exhibit obvious deterministic trends (see Figure 4-1), a test specification is chosen that includes intercepts but no linear trends in the cointegration equations and does not include deterministic trends in the level data of the endogenous variables. According to Johansen (1995) this can be expressed as:

$$\Pi z_{t-1} + B w_t = \alpha(\beta' z_{t-1} + \rho_0) \qquad 4.13$$

Next, the lag length p in Equation (4.2) has to be determined. Therefore unrestricted VARs of the underlying variables are estimated with lag orders of one to six and the optimal number of lags is determined based on different information criteria.[36] Balancing the implications of over-restricting the number of lags and failing to capture the actual dynamics with the implications of over-parameterizing the system and thus limiting the power of the cointegration test the approach follows the indication of the final prediction error, which suggests including two lags.

The results of the Johansen cointegration test with the specification discussed above are shown in Table 4-5. At a confidence level of 5% the trace test and the maximum eigenvalue test yield conflicting results of two versus one cointegration relationships, respectively. As the maximum eigenvalue test formulates a

---

36 The specifications are limited to a maximum of six lags to avoid over-parameterization against the background of the number of endogenous variables and the relatively short time period. The results are not reported here, however, they are made available upon request.

sharper alternative hypothesis than the trace test, it is assumed that only one cointegration relationship exists between the endogenous variables.

Table 4-5: Johansen cointegration test

Hypothe-sized no. of coin-tegration equa-tions	Ei-gen-value	Trace approach				Max-Eigen approach			
		Trace statistic		Critical value (5%)	Prob**	Max Eigen-statistic		Critical value (5%)	Prob**
None	0.570	250.367	*	169.599	0.000	108.825	*	53.188	0.000
At most 1	0.305	141.541	*	134.678	0.019	46.998		47.079	0.051
At most 2	0.267	94.544		103.847	0.176	40.000		40.957	0.064
At most 3	0.175	54.544		76.973	0.700	24.759		34.806	0.465
At most 4	0.112	29.784		54.079	0.916	15.390		28.588	0.789
At most 5	0.071	14.394		35.193	0.965	9.493		22.300	0.872
At most 6	0.028	4.901		20.262	0.984	3.610		15.892	0.974
At most 7	0.010	1.291		9.165	0.909	1.291		9.165	0.909

* Denotes rejection of hypothesis at the 5% confidence level
** MacKinnon *et al.* (1999) *p*-values

This table reports the results of the Johansen cointegration test for the endogenous variables CS_t, $Level_t$, $Slope_t$, $Convex_t$, Ret_t, $Vola_t$, $SWAP_t$, and CPI_t. The test uses a specification with intercepts and without trends in the cointegration equations and without deterministic trends in the endogenous variables. An exogenous dummy variable is included for the peak of the financial crisis (D_{crisis}) and the cointegration test is conducted with two lags in the first differences of the variables. * denotes a rejection of the hypothesis at a 5% significance level.

Based on these results an ECM with the same specification used for the cointegration test is estimated. It is assumed that one cointegration equation exists and the cointegration vector is normalized so that CS_t is expressed as a function of the other endogenous variables. Table 4-6 summarizes the parameter estimates of the ECM.

Table 4-6: Error correction model (Johansen approach)

Cointegration equation: Dependent variable is CS_{t-1}		
Constant	0.0079 (0.0029)	***
$Level_{t-1}$	-0.7034 (0.2335)	***
$Slope_{t-1}$	-0.5698 (0.1348)	***
$Convex_{t-1}$	0.2087 (0.2026)	
Ret_{t-1}	-0.0036 (0.0025)	
$Vola_{t-1}$	0.0218 (0.0053)	***
$Swap_{t-1}$	4.4169 (0.3324)	***
CPI_{t-1}	0.4281 (0.0696)	***

Error correction

Dependent variable:	ΔCS_t		$\Delta Slope_t$	
EC_{t-1}	-0.3284 (0.0462)	***	-0.0956 (0.0359)	***
ΔCS_{t-1}	0.3295 (0.1050)	***	0.0267 (0.0815)	
ΔCS_{t-2}	-0.3873 (0.1132)	***	-0.2302 (0.0878)	***
$\Delta Level_{t-1}$	0.8190 (0.2021)	***	-0.2752 (0.1568)	*
$\Delta Level_{t-2}$	0.3711 (0.2130)	*	0.3192 (0.1652)	*
$\Delta Slope_{t-1}$	0.4985 (0.1492)	***	-0.0029 (0.1157)	
$\Delta Slope_{t-2}$	-0.0265 (0.1564)		0.0686 (0.1213)	
$\Delta Convex_{t-1}$	-0.4967 (0.1435)	***	0.0838 (0.1113)	
$\Delta Convex_{t-2}$	-0.1868 (0.1488)		-0.2701 (0.1154)	**
ΔRet_{t-1}	-0.0009 (0.0021)		-0.0002 (0.0016)	
ΔRet_{t-2}	0.0023 (0.0020)		-0.0004 (0.0016)	
$\Delta Vola_{t-1}$	-0.0055 (0.0043)		0.0004 (0.0033)	
$\Delta Vola_{t-2}$	0.0087 (0.0044)	*	-0.0022 (0.0034)	
$\Delta Swap_{t-1}$	-0.1684 (0.4283)		0.2184 (0.3322)	
$\Delta Swap_{t-2}$	0.4883 (0.4249)		-0.0824 (0.3296)	
ΔCPI_{t-1}	-0.4041 (0.1087)	***	-0.0160 (0.0843)	
ΔCPI_{t-2}	-0.2117 (0.1122)	*	-0.0214 (0.0871)	
D_{crisis}	0.0058 (0.0009)	***	0.0033 (0.0007)	***
R-squared	0.6094		0.4030	
Adj. R-squared	0.5496		0.3115	
F-statistic	10.1877		4.4073	
Log likelihood	667.29		700.06	
Akaike info. criterion	-10.0665		-10.5745	
Schwarz info. criterion	-9.6674		-10.1755	

This table reports the estimates of the cointegration equation and the ECM for the endogenous variables CS_t, $Level_t$, $Slope_t$, $Convex_t$, Ret_t, $Vola_t$, $SWAP_t$, and CPI_t. The existence of one cointegration equation is assumed. The cointegration vector is normalized so that CS_t is expressed as function of the other endogenous variables. The model uses a specification with intercepts and without trends in the cointegration equations and without deterministic trends in the endogenous variables. An exogenous dummy variable is included for the peak of the financial crisis (D_{crisis}). The ECM is estimated with two lags in the first differences of the variables. Error corrections for the endogenous variables are only reported if the coefficient of the error correction term EC_t is significant and meaningful. *** (**, *) denotes significant parameters at a 1% (5%, 10%) significance level. Standard errors are reported in brackets.

The first part of Table 4-6 shows the estimated long-term relationship of Equation (4.12) with CS_t as dependent variable. Significant coefficients are found for all variables except $Convex_{t-1}$ and Ret_{t-1}.

As predicted by structural models, the risk-free yield ($Level_{t-1}$) is negatively related to credit spreads. Thus, the results support the findings of Pape and Schlecker (2007), which implies that credit spreads narrow with an increasing spot rate because the default probability of firms decreases.

In line with Miloudi and Moraux (2009), this study also finds that an increasing slope of the yield curve ($Slope_{t-1}$) leads to decreasing credit spreads. The negative relationship shows that the slope affects credit spreads in the same way as the spot rate. Hence, the theory is supported that an increasing slope of the yield curve reflects the expectation of a rising spot rate in the future.

Declining market liquidity, expressed as $Swap_{t-1}$, leads to a strong and significant widening of credit spreads. This reflects the preference of market participants for riskless government bonds vis-à-vis risky corporate bonds if liquidity in the corporate bond market dries up. The results underline the importance of liquidity in explaining the credit spread puzzle.[37]

While the effect is not statistically significant, the sign of the coefficient for Ret_{t-1} is correct. Increasing stock market returns generally imply an improving business climate, which leads to a deleveraging of companies and thus decreasing default probabilities and declining credit spreads. The results of a negative relationship are in line with Pape and Schlecker (2007), however deviate from those of Davies (2008), who finds a positive long-run relationship between the stock market and credit spreads.

The effect of increasing stock market volatility ($Vola_{t-1}$) is as structural models predict. Rising volatility increases option values and thus leads to decreasing bond prices and widening credit spreads.

Finally, the results also support the theory that increasing inflationary pressure (CPI_{t-1}) leads to rising credit spreads because risk premiums for corporate bond investments demanded by investors increase.

The second part of Table 4-6 shows the parameter estimates of the ECM. There are two significant and meaningful models that explain short-term adjustments to deviations of the endogenous variables from their equilibrium relationship.

The first model explains the short-term adjustments through changes in credit spreads. The corresponding error correction parameter, estimated as -0.33, is

---

[37] The credit spread puzzle implies that the observed yield differences between corporate bonds and government bonds are larger than the default risk premium of the corporate bonds (see e.g., Elton *et al.* (2001), or Hull *et al.* (2005)).

negative and highly significant. Approximately 33% of the disequilibrium converges back to the moving long-term equilibrium in the following month. The adjusted R-squared of 0.55 shows that the overall fit of this model is reasonably high because more than half of the variation in credit spreads can be explained by the included variables.

The second model shows that changes in the slope of the risk-free yield curve help to explain short-term corrections to deviations from the equilibrium between the endogenous variables. While the error correction parameter, estimated as -0.10, is smaller than the parameter of the first model in absolute terms, it is nevertheless significant and has the correct sign. The overall fit of the second model is also smaller than that of the first model. The adjusted R-squared of 0.31 shows that less than one-third of the credit spread variation is explained by the variables of the model. In addition, in the second model the number of significant coefficients of the lagged differences of the endogenous variables is smaller than in the first model.

Finally, both models have the fact in common, that the financial crisis dummy variable has a positive and highly significant coefficient. This shows that the financial crisis had a significant impact on the relationship between the endogenous variables. In the case of the credit spread model the positive parameter estimate shows that credit spread changes were significantly more pronounced during the peak of the financial crisis.

4.5.2 Results of ARDL Cointegration Test

The ARDL cointegration approach is started by estimating the UECM of Equation (4.6). Based on theoretical considerations CS_t is defined as the dependent variable y_t. The vector x_t contains the forcing variables $Level_t$, $Slope_t$, $Convex_t$, Ret_t, $Vola_t$, $SWAP_t$, and CPI_t; w_t contains a constant and the financial crisis dummy variable D_{crisis}. The Wald test of joint significance of all δ_i (i = 0, 1, 2, ..., 7) and the t-test of δ_0 are conducted for different lag orders p.

The results of the bounds tests are reported in Table 4-7. In addition to the asymptotic critical values for the Wald test given by Pesaran *et al.* (2001) critical values reported by Narayan (2005) for a sample size of 80 observations[38] are used to reflect the limited number of data points. As the sample size is larger than 80 observations, those critical values are even more restrictive than the sample requires. Up to a lag order of p = 5, all tests indicate that the computed

---

38 This is the maximum number of observations for which Narayan (2005) computes critical values.

test statistics are outside the upper bound at a 5% significance level. Hence, all variables are assumed to be purely I(1) and the hypothesis of no long-term relationship is conclusively rejected. If a lag order of $p = 6$ is chosen, the Wald tests still indicate the existence of a cointegration relationship irrespective of the choice of critical values. The t-test, however, is inconclusive because the computed t-value of -3.90 falls within the lower and the upper bound. This finding leads to set the maximum lag order to $p = 5$ for the following estimations.

Table 4-7: Bounds testing approach

No. of lags	F-statistic	t-statistic	Cointegration test		
			F_{crit} PSS*	F_{crit} N**	t_{crit} PSS***
1	11.28	-7.12	C	C	C
2	11.85	-8.57	C	C	C
3	9.51	-7.72	C	C	C
4	8.38	-7.29	C	C	C
5	7.66	-6.43	C	C	C
6	5.64	-3.90	C	C	I

*	Wald test with asymptotic 5% critical values according to Pesaran *et al.* (2001). The values for the lower bound and the upper bound are 2.32 and 3.50, respectively.
**	Wald test with 5% critical values for n = 80 according to Narayan (2005). The values for the lower bound and the upper bound are 2.48 and 3.75, respectively.
***	t-test with asymptotic 5% critical values according to Pesaran *et al.* (2001). The values for the lower bound and the upper bound are -2.86 and -4.57, respectively.

This table shows the results of the bounds testing approach for the existence of a long-term relationship between the dependent variable CS_t and the forcing variables $Level_t$, $Slope_t$, $Convex_t$, Ret_t, $Vola_t$, $SWAP_t$, and CPI_t. Test equations with an unrestricted intercept and without a linear trend (Case III in Pesaran et al. (2001)) are used. A dummy variable is included for the peak of the financial crisis (D_{crisis}) and the bounds test is conducted with different lag orders. In the last three columns C denotes that the computed test statistic is above the upper bound and the variables are cointegrated; NC denotes that the test statistic is below the lower bound and the variables are not cointegrated; I denotes that the test statistic is between the lower and the upper bound and the inference is inconclusive. Three tests for cointegration are conducted: a Wald test with asymptotic critical values provided by Pesaran et al. (2001), a Wald test with critical values for n = 80 provided by Narayan (2005), and a t-test with asymptotic critical values provided by Pesaran et al. (2001).

Having established that a long-term relationship between credit spreads and the forcing variables exists, the ARDL model of Equation (4.7) is estimated. Based on the AIC the model with the optimal lag distribution is chosen from $(5+1)^{7+1}$= 1679616 different estimations. The preferred model is an ARDL(1,3,4,5,0,1,2,3) specification with estimates of the long-run coefficients reported in Table 4-8.

All parameters in the long-term relationship of the variables are statistically significant at a 5% level and except for Ret_t also at a 1% level.

Comparing the ARDL estimates in Table 4-8 with the Johansen estimates of the long-run coefficients in Table 4-6, it becomes evident that all parameters have the same sign. Hence, the economic interpretation of the interdependencies between the variables given in section 4.5.1 also applies. The variables $Slope_t$, $Vola_t$, $SWAP_t$, and CPI_t have a comparable economic impact on credit spreads in both approaches and the coefficients do not deviate by more than 20%. However, the long-run coefficient of $Level_t$ is considerably larger in absolute terms than the coefficient estimated with the Johansen approach. Also, $Convex_t$ and Ret_t have a much larger impact on credit spreads in the ARDL approach, both economically and statistically. The main reason for these deviations is the flexibility of the ARDL approach, which allows selecting different lag orders for the variables. While the Johansen approach sets a common lag length to all variables, a very high number of five lags for $Convex_t$ and a very low number of zero lags for Ret_t are found to be most suitable for the ARDL estimation.

Table 4-8: Long-term relationship (ARDL approach)

Variable	Estimate		Std. err.	t-stat	Prob
Constant	0.0116	***	0.0029	3.9861	0.0001
$Level_t$	-1.3215	***	0.2627	-5.0307	0.0000
$Slope_t$	-0.6879	***	0.1356	-5.0732	0.0000
$Convex_t$	0.7438	***	0.2426	3.0664	0.0028
Ret_t	-0.0058	**	0.0023	-2.4900	0.0144
$Vola_t$	0.0199	***	0.0054	3.6541	0.0004
$Swap_t$	4.7212	***	0.3023	15.6175	0.0000
CPI_t	0.3729	***	0.0694	5.3739	0.0000

This table shows the estimates of the long-term relationship between the dependent variable CS_t and the forcing variables $Level_t$, $Slope_t$, $Convex_t$, Ret_t, $Vola_t$, $SWAP_t$. The coefficients are calculated from OLS estimates of an ARDL(1,3,4,5,0,1,2,3) model. Reported standard errors are computed using the delta method. *** (**, *) denotes significant parameters at a 1% (5%, 10%) significance level.

The short-term dynamics of the conditional ECM of Equation (4.10) associated with the estimated ARDL(1,3,4,5,0,1,2,3) specification are given in Table 4-9. The results reveal an error correction coefficient of -0.38, which is highly significant and even higher in absolute terms than estimated by the Johansen approach. The financial crisis dummy variable is statistically significant and has a positive sign as observed and explained in the Johansen approach. The adjusted R-squared of 0.82 is substantially higher than the adjusted R-squared in the Johansen approach. Furthermore, the regression passes several diagnostic tests. At conventional significance levels, non-normality, heteroscedasticity, and serial correlation of the residuals can be rejected and no evidence is found for mis-specification in the functional form.

Table 4-9: Error correction model (ARDL approach)

Variable	Estimate		Std. err.	t-stat	Prob
EC_{t-1}	-0.3780	***	0.0377	-10.0347	0.0000
$\Delta Level_t$	-0.2171		0.1551	-1.3998	0.1647
$\Delta Level_{t-1}$	0.7635	***	0.1502	5.0817	0.0000
$\Delta Level_{t-2}$	0.2330		0.1586	1.4692	0.1449
$\Delta Slope_t$	-0.1399		0.1072	-1.3054	0.1948
$\Delta Slope_{t-1}$	0.3263	***	0.1027	3.1757	0.0020
$\Delta Slope_{t-2}$	0.0365		0.1024	0.3561	0.7225
$\Delta Slope_{t-3}$	-0.4223	***	0.0824	-5.1263	0.0000
$\Delta Convex_t$	0.0384		0.1075	0.3570	0.7219
$\Delta Convex_{t-1}$	-0.4976	***	0.1122	-4.4355	0.0000
$\Delta Convex_{t-2}$	-0.1917	*	0.1141	-1.6805	0.0960
$\Delta Convex_{t-3}$	-0.1039	*	0.0567	-1.8333	0.0698
$\Delta Convex_{t-4}$	-0.0976	*	0.0538	-1.8140	0.0727
ΔRet_t	-0.0022	**	0.0010	-2.2270	0.0282
$\Delta Vola_t$	0.0178	***	0.0029	6.1175	0.0000
$\Delta Swap_t$	1.5233	***	0.2796	5.4485	0.0000
$\Delta Swap_{t-1}$	-0.6744	**	0.2770	-2.4342	0.0167
ΔCPI_t	-0.0444		0.0732	-0.6059	0.5460
ΔCPI_{t-1}	-0.3062	***	0.0753	-4.0651	0.0001
ΔCPI_{t-2}	-0.1185		0.0758	-1.5644	0.1209
D_{crisis}	0.0048	***	0.0007	6.8526	0.0000

$EC_t = CS_t + 1.32 Level_t + 0.69 Slope_t - 0.74 Convex_t + 0.01 Ret_t - 0.02 Vola_t - 4.72 SWAP_t$
$\quad - 0.37 CPI_t - 0.01$

Diagnostics			
R-squared	0.8581	Durbin-Watson statistic	2.1895
Adj. R-squared	0.8194	Mean dependent variable	0.0001
Std. err. of regression	0.0009	Std. dev. dependent variable	0.0022
Sum squared residuals	0.0001	Akaike info. criterion	-10.9036
Log likelihood	720.3791	Schwarz info. criterion	-10.2765

Residual and stability tests

$\chi_N^2(2)=0.9795$ [0.6128]; $\chi_{SC}^2(2)=1.9805$ [0.3715]; $\chi_H^2(1)=1.8353$ [0.1755]; $\chi_{FF}^2(1)=0.8919$ [0.3450]

This table shows the ECM for the dependent variable ΔCS_t using an ARDL(1,3,4,5,0,1,2,3) model. The error correction term EC_t is given by the residuals of the long-term relationship between CS_t and the forcing variables $Level_t$, $Slope_t$, $Convex_t$, Ret_t, $Vola_t$, $SWAP_t$, and CPI_t. Reported standard errors are computed using the delta method. *** (**, *) denotes significant parameters at a 1% (5%, 10%) significance level. $\chi_N^2(2)$, $\chi_{SC}^2(2)$, $\chi_H^2(1)$, and $\chi_{FF}^2(1)$ denote Chi-squared statistics for the Jarque-Bera test for normality of the residuals, the Breusch-Godfrey test for no residual serial correlation, the ARCH test for homoscedasticity, and the Ramsey RESET test for no misspecification in the functional form; p-values are given in [ ].

Figure 4-2 demonstrates that the model implied credit spreads have a very good fit and the residuals are only at few points outside the two standard error bands.

Figure 4-2: Actual and fitted credit spreads

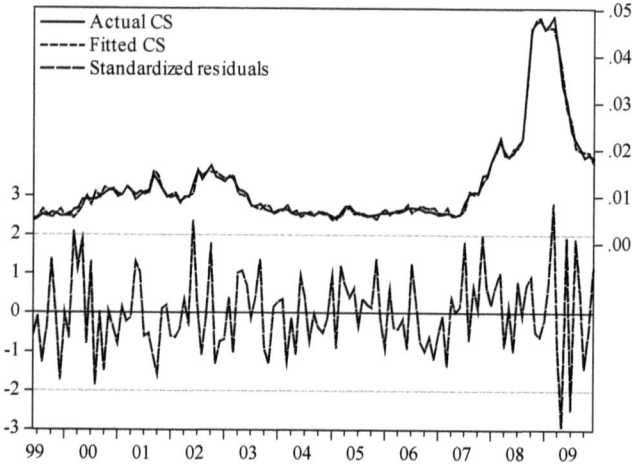

This figure shows on the right axis actual credit spreads and fitted credit spreads based on the estimated ECM using an ARDL(1,3,4,5,0,1,2,3) model. On the left axis standardized residuals are plotted with two standard error bands.

Overall, this leads to the conclusion that the ARDL approach is well suited to describe the interdependencies between credit spreads and the forcing variables. Comparing the results of the Johansen approach with the results of the ARDL approach it can be concluded that the second has a better fit due to its advantages described above.

4.5.3 Deviations of Credit Spreads from Equilibrium

The long-term relationships that result from the cointegration approaches can be interpreted as moving equilibriums between the endogenous variables. Hence, under the assumption that credit spreads are a function of the other (forcing) variables, the residuals in Equation (4.12) express the deviations of observed credit spreads from equilibrium credit spreads. A positive sign implies that actual credit spreads (actual bond prices) are above (below) equilibrium based on the long-term relationship with the forcing variables.

Figure 4-3: Deviations of actual credit spreads from long-term equilibrium

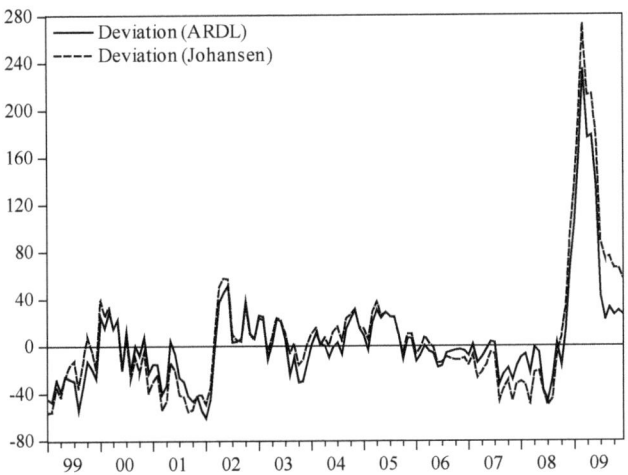

This figure shows the deviation of actual credit spreads from equilibrium that is estimated by the cointegration relationship between CS_t and the forcing variables $Level_t$, $Slope_t$, $Convex_t$, Ret_t, $Vola_t$, $SWAP_t$, and CPI_t. A positive (negative) sign means that actual credit spreads are above (below) the estimated equilibrium. The plotted deviations are expressed in basis points.

Figure 4-3 shows the deviations of actual credit spreads from equilibrium estimated by the Johansen and the ARDL approaches. Between January 1999 and September 2008 deviations of actual credit spreads from their long-run equilibrium were relatively small. The observed credit spreads are never more than 60 basis points above or below the long-term estimate and disequilibriums are adjusted very quickly in the months following the mismatch. This observation coincides with the high error correction coefficients described above.

The only notable exception to this observation is the period after September 2008. After the collapse of Lehman Brothers, credit spreads surged and the increase was well beyond levels explained by the economic variables of the models. Actual credit spreads were up to 270 basis points and 230 basis points above the equilibrium value predicted by the Johansen approach and the ARDL approach, respectively. Furthermore, there is no immediate convergence towards equilibrium after September 2008, but the over-valuation of credit spreads increases between October 2008 and March 2009. Actual credit spreads only converge back towards equilibrium after April 2009. Towards the end of the sample period credit spreads have approached their long-term equilibrium. While the Johansen approach still predicts an over-pricing of credit spreads by approximately 65 basis points in December 2009, the ARDL approach estimates that credit spreads are above equilibrium by merely 30 basis points.

4.6 Conclusion

This study conducts a cointegration analysis of credit spreads for the European corporate bond market in order to test for the existence of a long-term relationship between credit spreads and a number of variables that theoretical and empirical literature suggests as determinants for corporate bond prices and credit spreads.

The results show that cointegration analysis is suited to describe the volatile movement of credit spreads in the European corporate bond market during the last decade. Both the Johansen and the ARDL cointegration approach suggest that a long-term relationship between credit spreads and the forcing variables exists, so that neglecting this relationship would yield misleading and probably biased results.

In the long-run, the interdependencies between credit spreads and their determinants are as existing literature predicts. While this study finds support for negative relationships between credit spreads and the risk-free rate, the slope of the yield curve, and the equity market return, positive relationships exist between credit spreads and the convexity of the yield curve, the equity volatility, the illiquidity of the corporate bond market, and the inflation. The ARDL approach yields statistically significant estimates of the long-term impacts of all forcing variables on credit spreads, whereas the equity market return and the convexity have no significant long-term impacts in the Johansen approach.

Error correction models of both cointegration approaches indicate a highly significant and strong convergence towards the long-term equilibrium between the endogenous variables. The Johansen approach and the ARDL approach predict that disequilibriums adjust towards the long-term relationship in the following month by 33% and 38%, respectively. Overall, the fit of both error correction models is good. The adjusted R-squared for the Johansen approach reaches 55% and in the ARDL approach it is even 82%.

Comparing the results of the Johansen approach with the results of the ARDL approach, the second is preferred because it is more flexible, the assumptions are less restrictive, and the overall fit is better.

Finally, actual credit spreads are compared with equilibrium credit spreads predicted by the long-term relationship between the endogenous variables. The theory is supported that capital markets significantly over-reacted after the collapse of Lehman Brothers in September 2008. Although a variable for market-wide illiquidity of corporate bonds is included, actual credit spreads were more than 200 basis points above the model implied equilibrium and the disequilibrium was only slowly adjusted. Towards the end of 2009, however, a convergence of credit spreads towards equilibrium can be observed, which indicates that capital markets have almost returned to their pre-crisis assessment of risk inherent in the corporate bond market.

Conclusion

This thesis examines in detail and from different angles what determines credit spread variations in the European corporate bond market. To understand the key determinants of credit spreads is important for corporates, banks and other financial institutions, investors and portfolio managers, regulators, and policy makers. Nevertheless, existing studies of credit spreads focus mainly on the U.S. market, omit important variables such as market-wide or bond-specific liquidity, fail to explain large parts of credit spread variations due to the applied methodology, or study only short-term dynamics of credit spread changes while neglecting long-term relationships. Furthermore, the recent financial crisis caused a significant widening of credit spreads across all sectors and all credit qualities. To understand the impact of the crisis on the interdependencies between economic variables and credit spreads is an important issue for researchers and practitioners alike.

This thesis addresses these shortcomings of the existing empirical literature with three self-contained empirical studies by exploring the following overall research topics. First, the linkages between macroeconomic factors and the term structure of credit spreads are analyzed and the question whether the European corporate bond market is integrated is addressed. Second, the impact of liquidity on credit spreads is examined and the effect of the financial crisis on the liquidity risk of corporate bonds is explored for different sectors and credit qualities. Third, the long-term and short-term relationships between credit spreads and their determinants are analyzed and disequilibriums during the financial crisis are evaluated.

The findings of the three studies with regard to the research topics above are summarized in the following. The first study tests a macro-finance term structure model of credit spreads for the European corporate bond market. With this approach the maturity-related variation of credit spreads is specifically addressed because the whole term structure of credit spreads is analyzed and credit spread curves that are structurally linked by no-arbitrage rules are explained. In addition to latent factors, observable factors that are linked to the macroeconomic variables inflation, real activity, and financial activity are included.

By comparing the results of the study with the results of a similar study for the U.S. market, which is seen as a benchmark regarding the level of financial integration, the study indirectly examines the degree of integration of the European bond market.

Evidence suggests that the European bond market is largely integrated, since the results of the European term structure model overall are in line with similar models tested for the U.S. market and credit spreads consistently react to the common underlying risk factors. Hence, the study concludes that the basic principle of the law of one price seems to hold to a large extent for European corporate bonds.

However, several deviations in the structure of the results compared to the results of the U.S. term structure model estimated by Amato and Luisi (2006) indicate that financial integration in Europe is still below levels observed in the U.S. A detailed analysis of the market price of risk shows that not all factors of the model contribute uniformly to the risk premiums. In addition, the curvatures of the credit spread curves are not accurately explained by latent factors. These findings are in contrast to Amato and Luisi's (2006) results and one explanation for this is that residual segmentation in the European bond market leads to partial deviations of the law of one price.

In order to establish the comparability to the U.S. model of Amato and Luisi (2006), the first study omits liquidity as an additional risk factor. An analysis of the latent variables, however, shows that an omitted macroeconomic factor seems to have a systematic impact on credit spreads across all rating categories. One explanation for this observation could be that credit spreads react to changes in market liquidity, especially during the recent financial crisis.

Following this hypothesis, the second study addresses the question how liquidity relates to credit spreads in the European corporate bond market and whether the liquidity risk has changed during the financial crisis.

Different panel regressions on a sample of European corporate bonds yield that changes in bond-specific and market-wide liquidity have an economically and statistically significant impact on credit spread changes. Thus, theoretical considerations that liquidity risk premiums in bond prices help to explain the credit spread puzzle are confirmed. In addition, the hypothesis that liquidity risk has increased during the recent financial crisis is supported by a structural break analysis. Evidence shows that during the financial crisis the impact of changes in bond-specific liquidity and market-wide liquidity on credit spread changes has increased by over 100% and about 200%, respectively. In contrast, typical variables measuring increased credit risk, such as rating deterioration or rising leverage, do not have a significant impact on credit spread changes. Hence, the hypothesis that credit spreads have increased during the crisis due to declining liquidity and not because of increased credit risk can be confirmed.

Furthermore, the second study differentiates between industry sectors (financial institutions and non-financial corporates) and the credit quality (high-rated bonds and low-rated bonds). Overall, the findings suggest that high-rated bonds and bonds of financial institutions have a much higher exposure to liquidity risk during the financial crisis than low-rated bonds and bonds of non-financial corporates. While markets already priced-in illiquidity premiums for bonds with lower credit quality and bonds of non-financial corporates before the start of the financial crisis, liquidity risk has become relevant for high-rated bonds and bonds of financial institutions only during the financial crisis. This finding is especially relevant for the development of the regulatory framework for banks, which attaches little weight to liquidity risk in its current version. A revision of the framework to require banks to hold more capital for liquidity risk especially for asset classes with low credit risk seems prudent.

Most existing studies on credit spreads only analyze the short-term dynamics. Besides the low power of most models to explain credit spread variations, omitting the long-term relationship between variables that are linked by cointegration relations can lead to biased results (Duan and Pliska (2004)). To address the question whether credit spreads are linked to a set of determining variables via a long-term relationship, the third study conducts a cointegration analysis on European corporate credit spreads.

Two different cointegration approaches, the Johansen procedure and the ARDL procedure, confirm the existence of a long-term relationship between credit spreads and variables that are linked to the term structure of the risk-free interest rate, the equity market, market liquidity, and inflation. The choice of a broad set of factors that simultaneously interact with credit spreads considerably extends previous cointegration studies, which mainly analyze the partial relationships between credit spreads and selected variables. Overall, the ARDL approach is preferred to the Johansen approach because of the better fit and its higher flexibility in capturing the dynamics of the variables. Furthermore, it has less restrictive assumptions.

The existence of a long-term relationship between European credit spreads and their determinants is an important finding, as it suggests that different markets, such as the government bond market and the equity market, and economic variables, such as liquidity and inflation, are interlinked with the corporate bond market.

Error correction models that capture both the long-term relationship and the short-term dynamics of the endogenous variables are able to explain large parts of credit spread variations. The models show that deviations from equilibrium are balanced by the short-term dynamics of the variables and approximately one-third of the disequilibriums between credit spreads and their determinants is adjusted in the subsequent month.

Finally, an analysis of equilibrium credit spreads that are derived from the estimated long-term relationship between the endogenous variables yields that actual credit spreads were significantly above equilibrium after the collapse of Lehman Brothers in September 2008. Even after accounting for market-wide illiquidity of corporate bonds, actual credit spreads were more than 200 basis points above the equilibrium spreads predicted by the different models. Actual credit spreads only converge back to the estimated equilibrium at the end of 2009.

This thesis provides a comprehensive analysis of the determinants of credit spreads for the European corporate bond market. It is shown that macroeconomic factors, credit risk factors related to the bond issuer, and liquidity risk factors are major drivers for spreads of corporate bond yields over riskless government bond yields. Furthermore, the thesis confirms that the dynamics of credit spreads are determined by long-term and short-term relationships.

Future research could extend the scope of these findings to other asset classes that are subject to default risk. With increasing data availability the dynamics of European credit spreads in the high yield sector should be examined and differences between the determinants of investment grade credit spreads and high yield credit spreads should be explored. Another extension to the findings of this thesis could be to analyze and compare the determinants of credit spreads of defaultable government bonds with those of corporate bonds. The significant widening of spreads on Greek government bonds during the recent financial crisis has put Greece and the whole euro area at risk of a collapse. However, the actual causal relations between the underlying economic situation of Greece, speculative market forces, and instruments such as credit default swaps, remain unclear. Future research in this area is needed to understand the dynamics of such a crisis and give recommendations to policy makers as to how to deal with and intervene in similar situations in the future.

References

Acharya, V. V., & Pedersen, L. H. (2005). Asset Pricing with Liquidity Risk. *Journal of Financial Economics*, 77(2), 375-410.

Amato, J. D., & Luisi, M. (2006). *Macro Factors in the Term Structure of Credit Spreads*. Bank for International Settlement, Working Paper No. 203.

Amato, J. D., & Remolona, E. M. (2003). The Credit Spread Puzzle. *BIS Quarterly Review*, 51-63.

Amihud, Y., & Mendelson, H. (1986). Asset Pricing and the Bid-Ask Spread. *Journal of Financial Economics*, 17(2), 223-249.

Amihud, Y., & Mendelson, H. (1991). Liquidity, Maturity, and the Yields on U.S. Treasury Securities. *Journal of Finance*, 46(4), 1411-1425.

Ang, A., & Piazzesi, M. (2003). A No-Arbitrage Vector Autoregression of Term Structure Dynamics with Macroeconomic and Latent Variables. *Journal of Monetary Economics*, 50(4), 745-787.

Arora, N., Bohn, J. R., & Zhu, F. (2005). Reduced Form vs. Structural Models of Credit Risk: A Case Study of Three Models. *Journal of Investment Management*, 3(4), 43-67.

Athanassakos, G., & Carayannopoulos, P. (2001). An Empirical Analysis of the Relationship of Bond Yield Spreads and Macro-economic Factors. *Applied Financial Economics*, 11(2), 197-207.

Baele, L., Ferrando, A., Hördahl, P., Krylova, E., & Monnet, C. (2004). Measuring European Financial Integration. *Oxford Review of Economic Policy*, 20(4), 509-530.

Balli, F. (2009). Spillover Effects on Government Bond Yields in Euro Zone. Does Full Financial Integration Exist in European Government Bond Markets? *Journal of Economics & Finance*, 33(4), 331-363.

Baltagi, B. H. (2008). *Econometric Analysis of Panel Data* (4. ed.). Chichester: Wiley.

Banerjee, A., Dolado, J., & Mestre, R. (1998). Error-correction Mechanism Tests for Cointegration in a Single-equation Framework. *Journal of Time Series Analysis*, 19(3), 267-283.

Banerjee, A., & Russell, B. (2001). The Relationship between the Markup and Inflation in the G7 Economies and Australia. *Review of Economics and Statistics*, 83(2), 377-384.

Bansal, R., & Zhou, H. (2002). Term Structure of Interest Rates with Regime Shifts. *Journal of Finance*, 57(5), 1997-2043.

Basel Committee on Banking Supervision. (2006). *Basel II: International Convergence of Capital Measurement and Capital Standards: A Revised Framework - Comprehensive Version.* Bank for International Settlements.

Black, F., & Cox, J. C. (1976). Valuing Corporate Securities: Some Effects of Bond Indenture Provisions. *Journal of Finance*, 31(2), 351-367.

Black, F., & Scholes, M. (1973). The Pricing of Options and Corporate Liabilities. *Journal of Political Economy*, 81(3), 637-654.

Bolder, D. J. (2001). *Affine Term-Structure Models: Theory and Implementation.* Bank of Canada, Working Paper 2001-15.

Boss, M., & Scheicher, M. (2002). The Determinants of Credit Spread Changes in the Euro Area. *Bank for International Settlements Papers*, 12, 181-199.

Boudoukh, J., & Whitelaw, R. F. (1993). Liquidity as a Choice Variable: A Lesson from the Japanese Government Bond Market. *Review of Financial Studies*, 6(2), 265-292.

Brennan, M. J., & Subrahmanyam, A. (1996). Market Microstructure and Asset Pricing: On the Compensation for Illiquidity in Stock Returns. *Journal of Financial Economics*, 41(3), 441-464.

Broyden, C. G. (1970). The Convergence of a Class of Double-rank Minimization Algorithms 1. General Considerations. *IMA Journal of Applied Mathematics*, 6(1), 76-90.

Brunnermeier, M. K. (2009). Deciphering the Liquidity and Credit Crunch 2007-2008. *Journal of Economic Perspectives*, 23(1), 77-100.

Campello, M., Chen, L., & Zhang, L. (2008). Expected Returns, Yield Spreads, and Asset Pricing Tests. *Review of Financial Studies*, 21(3), 1297-1338.

Castagnetti, C., & Rossi, E. (2008). *Euro Corporate Bonds Risk Factors.* MPRA, Paper No. 13440.

Chen, L., Collin-Dufresne, P., & Goldstein, R. S. (2009). On the Relation Between the Credit Spread Puzzle and the Equity Premium Puzzle. *Review of Financial Studies*, 22(9), 3367-3409.

Chen, L., Lesmond, D. A., & Wei, J. (2007). Corporate Yield Spreads and Bond Liquidity. *Journal of Finance*, 62(1), 119-149.

Chordia, T., Roll, R., & Subrahmanyam, A. (2001). Market Liquidity and Trading Activity. *Journal of Finance*, 56(2), 501-530.

Chordia, T., Sarkar, A., & Subrahmanyam, A. (2005). An Empirical Analysis of Stock and Bond Market Liquidity. *Review of Financial Studies*, 18(1), 85-129.

Chow, G. C. (1960). Tests of Equality Between Sets of Coefficients in Two Linear Regressions. *Econometrica*, 28(3), 591-605.

Collin-Dufresne, P., & Goldstein, R. S. (2001). Do Credit Spreads Reflect Stationary Leverage Ratios? *Journal of Finance*, 56(5), 1929-1957.

Collin-Dufresne, P., Goldstein, R. S., & Martin, J. S. (2001). The Determinants of Credit Spread Changes. *Journal of Finance*, 56(6), 2177-2207.

Cossin, D., & Pirotte, H. (2001). *Advanced Credit Risk Analysis. Financial Approaches and Mathematical Models to Assess, Price, and Manage Credit Risk*. Chichester: Wiley.

Covitz, D., & Downing, C. (2007). Liquidity or Credit Risk? The Determinants of Very Short-Term Corporate Yield Spreads. *Journal of Finance*, 62(5), 2303-2328.

Cox, J. C., Ingersoll, J. E., Jr., & Ross, S. A. (1985). A Theory of the Term Structure of Interest Rates. *Econometrica*, 53(2), 385-407.

Dai, Q., & Singleton, K. J. (2000). Specification Analysis of Affine Term Structure Models. *Journal of Finance*, 55(5), 1943-1978.

Date, P., & Wang, C. (2009). Linear Gaussian Affine Term Structure Models with Unobservable Factors: Calibration and Yield Forecasting. *European Journal of Operational Research*, 195(1), 156-166.

Davies, A. (2008). Credit Spread Determinants: An 85 Year Perspective. *Journal of Financial Markets*, 11(2), 180-197.

De Bondt, G. (2002). *Euro Area Corporate Debt Securities Market: First Empirical Evidence*. European Central Bank, Working Paper No. 164.

De Jong, F., & Driessen, J. (2006). *Liquidity Risk Premia in Corporate Bond Markets*. Tilburg University and University of Amsterdam, Working Paper.

Dewachter, H., & Lyrio, M. (2006). Macro Factors and the Term Structure of Interest Rates. *Journal of Money, Credit and Banking*, 38(1), 119-140.

Diaz, A., & Navarro, E. (2002). Yield Spread and Term to Maturity: Default vs. Liquidity. *European Financial Management*, 8(4), 449-477.

Diebold, F. X., Rudebusch, G. D., & Boragan Aruoba, S. (2006). The Macroeconomy and the Yield Curve: A Dynamic Latent Factor Approach. *Journal of Econometrics*, 131(1/2), 309-338.

Dionne, G., Gauthier, G., Hammami, K., Maurice, M., & Simonato, J.-G. (2007). *A Reduced Form Model of Default Spreads with Markov Switching Macroeconomic Factors*. CIRPEE, Working Paper 07-41.

Duan, J.-C., & Pliska, S. R. (2004). Option Valuation with Co-Integrated Asset Prices. *Journal of Economic Dynamics and Control*, 28(4), 727-754.

Duffee, G. R. (1998). The Relation Between Treasury Yields and Corporate Bond Yield Spreads. *Journal of Finance*, 53(6), 2225-2241.

Duffie, D., & Kan, R. (1996). A Yield-Factor Model of Interest Rates. *Mathematical Finance*, 6(4), 379-406.

Duffie, D., & Singleton, K. J. (1999). Modeling Term Structures of Defaultable Bonds. *Review of Financial Studies*, 12(4), 687-720.

Edwards, A. K., Harris, L. E., & Piwowar, M. S. (2007). Corporate Bond Market Transaction Costs and Transparency. *Journal of Finance*, 62(3), 1421-1451.

Elton, E. J., & Green, T. C. (1998). Tax and Liquidity Effects in Pricing Government Bonds. *Journal of Finance*, 53(5), 1533-1562.

Elton, E. J., Gruber, M. J., Agrawal, D., & Mann, C. (2001). Explaining the Rate Spread on Corporate Bonds. *Journal of Finance*, 56(1), 247-277.

Engle, R. F., & Granger, C. W. J. (1987). Co-integration and Error Correction: Representation, Estimation, and Testing. *Econometrica*, 55(2), 251-276.

Ericsson, J., & Renault, O. (2006). Liquidity and Credit Risk. *Journal of Finance*, 61(5), 2219-2250.

Fama, E. F., & French, K. R. (1993). Common Risk Factors in the Returns on Stocks and Bonds. *Journal of Financial Economics*, 33(1), 3-56.

Fernández, R. B. (1981). A Methodological Note on the Estimation of Time Series. *Review of Economics and Statistics*, 63(3), 471-476.

Fleming, M. J. (2003). Measuring Treasury Market Liquidity. *Economic Policy Review*, 9(3), 83-108.

Fletcher, R. (1970). A New Approach to Variable Metric Algorithms. *The Computer Journal*, 13(3), 317-322.

Goldfarb, D. (1970). A Family of Variable-Metric Methods Derived by Variational Means. *Mathematics of Computation*, 24(109), 23-26.

Goldreich, D., Hanke, B., & Nath, P. (2005). The Price of Future Liquidity: Time-Varying Liquidity in the U.S. Treasury Market. *Review of Finance*, 9(1), 1-32.

Haugen, R. A., & Baker, N. L. (1996). Commonality in the Determinants of Expected Stock Returns. *Journal of Financial Economics*, 41(3), 401-439.

Hördahl, P., Tristani, O., & Vestin, D. (2006). A Joint Econometric Model of Macroeconomic and Term-Structure Dynamics. *Journal of Econometrics*, 131(1-2), 405-444.

Houweling, P., Mentink, A., & Vorst, T. (2005). Comparing Possible Proxies of Corporate Bond Liquidity. *Journal of Banking & Finance*, 29(6), 1331-1358.

Hull, J. C., Predescu, M., & White, A. (2005). The Credit Spread Puzzle. *Journal of Financial Transformation*, 13, 131-134.

Hull, J. C., & White, A. (2000). Valuing Credit Default Swaps I: No Counterparty Default Risk. *Journal of Derivatives*, 8(1), 29-40.

Jarrow, R. A., & Turnbull, S. M. (1995). Pricing Derivatives on Financial Securities Subject to Credit Risk. *Journal of Finance*, 50(1), 53-85.

Johansen, S. (1991). Estimation and Hypothesis Testing of Cointegration Vectors in Gaussian Vector Autoregressive Models. *Econometrica*, 59(6), 1551-1580.

Johansen, S. (1995). *Likelihood-Based Inference in Cointegrated Vector Autoregressive Models*. Oxford: Oxford University Press.

Joutz, F., Mansi, S. A., & Maxwell, W. F. (2001). *The Dynamics of Corporate Credit Spreads*. Texas Tech University, Working Paper.

Kamara, A. (1994). Liquidity, Taxes, and Short-Term Treasury Yields. *Journal of Financial and Quantitative Analysis*, 29(3), 403-417.

Krishnamurthy, A. (2002). The Bond/Old-Bond Spread. *Journal of Financial Economics*, 66(2-3), 463-506.

Krishnan, C. N. V., Ritchken, P. H., & Thomson, J. B. (2007). *On Forecasting the Term Structure of Credit Spreads*. Federal Reserve Bank of Cleveland, Working Paper 07-05.

Leland, H. E. (1994). Corporate Debt Value, Bond Covenants, and Optimal Capital Structure. *Journal of Finance*, 49(4), 1213-1252.

Lemke, W. (2008). An Affine Macro-Finance Term Structure Model for the Euro Area. *North American Journal of Economics and Finance*, 19(1), 41-69.

Longstaff, F. A., Mithal, S., & Neis, E. (2005). Corporate Yield Spreads: Default Risk or Liquidity? New Evidence from the Credit Default Swap Market. *Journal of Finance*, 60(5), 2213-2253.

Longstaff, F. A., & Schwartz, E. S. (1992). Interest Rate Volatility and the Term Structure: A Two-Factor General Equilibrium Model. *Journal of Finance*, 47(4), 1259-1282.

Longstaff, F. A., & Schwartz, E. S. (1995). A Simple Approach to Valuing Risky Fixed and Floating Rate Debt. *Journal of Finance*, 50(3), 789-819.

Lütkepohl, H. (1991). *Introduction to Multiple Time Series Analysis*. New York; Berlin; London and Tokyo: Springer.

MacKinnon, J. G. (1996). Numerical Distribution Functions for Unit Root and Cointegration Tests. *Journal of Applied Econometrics*, 11(6), 601-618.

MacKinnon, J. G., Haug, A. A., & Michelis, L. (1999). Numerical Distribution Functions of Likelihood Ratio Tests for Cointegration. *Journal of Applied Econometrics*, 14(5), 563-577.

Mahanti, S., Nashikkar, A., Subrahmanyam, M., Chacko, G., & Mallik, G. (2008). Latent Liquidity: A New Measure of Liquidity, with an Application to Corporate Bonds. *Journal of Financial Economics*, 88(2), 272-298.

Merkus, H. R., Pollock, D. S. G., & de Vos, A. F. (1993). A Synopsis of the Smoothing Formulae Associated with the Kalman Filter. *Computational Economics*, 6(3-4), 177-200.

Merton, R. C. (1974). On the Pricing of Corporate Debt: The Risk Structure of Interest Rates. *Journal of Finance*, 29(2), 449-470.

Miloudi, A., & Moraux, F. (2009). Relations between Corporate Credit Spreads, Treasury Yields and the Equity Market. *International Journal of Business*, 14(2), 105-122.

Narayan, P. K. (2005). The Saving and Investment Nexus for China: Evidence from Cointegration Tests. *Applied Economics*, 37(17), 1979-1990.

Neal, R., Rolph, D. S., & Morris, C. (2000). *Interest Rates and Credit Spread Dynamics*. Federal Reserve Bank of Kansas City, Working Paper.

Nelson, C. R., & Siegel, A. F. (1987). Parsimonious Modeling of Yield Curves. *Journal of Business*, 60(4), 473-489.

Pagano, M., & von Thadden, E.-L. (2004). The European Bond Markets under EMU. *Oxford Review of Economic Policy*, 20(4), 531-554.

Pape, U., & Schlecker, M. (2007). *Are Credit Spreads and Interest Rates Co-Integrated? Empirical Analysis in the USD Corporate Bond Market*. ESCP-EAP Working Paper No. 25.

Pesaran, B., & Pesaran, M. H. (2009). *Time Series Econometrics using Microfit 5.0*. Oxford: Oxford University Press.

Pesaran, M. H., & Shin, Y. (1999). An Autoregressive Distributed-Lag Modelling Approach to Cointegration Analysis. Chapter 11. In S. Strom (Ed.), *Econometrics and Economic Theory in the 20th Century: The Ragnar Frisch Centennial Symposium*. Cambridge: Cambridge University Press.

Pesaran, M. H., Shin, Y., & Smith, R. J. (2001). Bounds Testing Approaches to the Analysis of Level Relationships. *Journal of Applied Econometrics*, 16(3), 289-326.

Piazzesi, M. (2009). Affine Term Structure Models. In Y. Ait-Sahalia & L. P. Hansen (Eds.), *Handbook of Financial Econometrics - Tools and Techniques*. Amsterdam: Elsevier.

Rottmann, H., & Seitz, F. (2008). Credit Spreads und ihre Determinanten: Eine empirische Analyse für Deutschland. *Kredit und Kapital*, 41(1), 59-78.

Rudebusch, G. D., Swanson, E. T., & Wu, T. (2006). The Bond Yield 'Conundrum' from a Macro-Finance Perspective. *Monetary and Economic Studies*, 24(S1), 83-109.

Rudebusch, G. D., & Wu, T. (2008). A Macro-finance Model of the Term Structure, Monetary Policy and the Economy. *Economic Journal*, 118(530), 906-926.

Russell, B., & Banerjee, A. (2008). The Long-Run Phillips Curve and Non-Stationary Inflation. *Journal of Macroeconomics*, 30(4), 1792-1815.

Shanno, D. F. (1970). Conditioning of Quasi-Newton Methods for Function Minimization. *Mathematics of Computation*, 24(111), 647-656.

Takahashi, A., Kobayashi, T., & Nakagawa, N. (2001). Pricing Convertible Bonds with Default Risk. *Journal of Fixed Income*, 11(3), 20.

Taylor, J. B. (1993). Discretion versus Policy Rules in Practice. *Carnegie-Rochester Conference Series on Public Policy*, 39, 195-214.

Taylor, J. B., & Williams, J. C. (2009). A Black Swan in the Money Market. *American Economic Journal: Macroeconomics*, 1(1), 58-83.

Terazzan, O. (2006). Estimating the Term Structure of Credit Spreads on Euro-Denominated Corporate Bonds. *Economic Notes*, 35(3), 355-375.

Van Landschoot, A. (2004). *Determinants of Euro Term Structure of Credit Spreads*. European Central Bank, Working Paper Series: 397.

Van Landschoot, A. (2008). Determinants of Yield Spread Dynamics: Euro versus US Dollar Corporate Bonds. *Journal of Banking and Finance*, 32(12), 2597-2605.

Vasicek, O. (1977). An Equilibrium Characterization of the Term Structure. *Journal of Financial Economics*, 5(2), 177-188.

Vayanos, D. (1998). Transactions Costs and Asset Prices: A Dynamic Equilibrium Model. *Review of Financial Studies*, 11(1), 1-58.

White, H. (1980). A Heteroskedasticity-Consistent Covariance Matrix Estimator and a Direct Test for Heteroskedasticity. *Econometrica*, 48(4), 817-838.

Wooldridge, J. M. (2007). *Econometric Analysis of Cross Section and Panel Data*. London: MIT Press.

Wu, L., & Zhang, F. X. (2005). *A No-Arbitrage Analysis of Economic Determinants of the Credit Spread Term Structure*. Federal Reserve Board Washington D.C., FEDS Discussion Paper No. 2005-59.

Zhang, B. Y., Zhou, H., & Zhu, H. (2009). Explaining Credit Default Swap Spreads with the Equity Volatility and Jump Risks of Individual Firms. *Review of Financial Studies*, 22(12), 5099-5131.

Zivot, E., & Andrews, D. W. K. (1992). Further Evidence on the Great Crash, the Oil-Price Shock, and the Unit-Root Hypothesis. *Journal of Business & Economic Statistics*, 10(3), 251-270.

Corporate Finance and Governance

Herausgegeben von Dirk Schiereck

Band 1   Sebastian Michael Gläsner: Return Patterns of German Open-End Real Estate Funds. An Empirical Explanation of Smooth Fund Returns. 2010.

Band 2   Patrick Ams: Directors' Dealings and Insider Trading in Germany. An Empirical Analysis. 2010.

Band 3   Joachim Vogt: Value Creation within the Construction Industry. A Study of Strategic Takeovers. 2011.

Band 4   Fabian Braemisch: Underpricing, Long-Run Performance, and Valuation of Initial Public Offerings. 2011.

Band 5   Matthäus Markus Sielecki: Creating and Governing an Integrated Market for Retail Banking Services in Europe. A Conceptual-Empirical Study of the Role of Regulation in Promoting a Single Euro Payments Area. 2011.

Band 6   Arne Wilkes: Determinants of Credit Spreads. An Empirical Analysis for the European Corporate Bond Market. 2011.

www.peterlang.de

www.ingramcontent.com/pod-product-compliance
Ingram Content Group UK Ltd.
Pitfield, Milton Keynes, MK11 3LW, UK
UKHW022154230426
12049UKWH00004BA/94